Book Synopsis

"FIVEFOLD OPERATIONS VOLUME TWO: Shifting Into Vision Casting & Team Building." This is the second volume of a series of fivefold ministry paradigms written to assist ministers and ministries with understanding that they are the fivefold blueprint and that the time is NOW for vision casting a fivefold ministry. Volume two:

- Provides revelation on how to write, pray, plant, cultivate, plow, build, and advance a vision, and how to create measurable blueprint goals.
- Equips ministers and ministries with insights on how to choose, train and equip team members as vision carriers, while also identifying and establishing them in their own destinies and callings.
- Trains vision carriers for warfare, how to drink their own cup of destiny and how to be bloodline breakers, who journey in a life of fulfilled and balanced destiny and purpose.

Please know that you will not only learn these operations, but how to establish them in a fivefold ministry. The answers you have been seeking awaits you. You are the fivefold blueprint so get to reading and building. **SHIFT! SHIFT RIGHT NOW!**

Kingdomshifterscec@gmail.com

Kingdomshifters.com

Connect with Taquetta via Facebook or YouTube

All rights reserved. This book is protected by the copyright laws of the United States of America. This book may not be reprinted for commercial gain or profit. The use of occasional page copying for personal or group study is permitted and encouraged. Permission will be granted upon request. Copyright 2019 – Kingdom Shifters Ministries

Taquetta's Ministry Bio

Dr. Apostle Taquetta Baker is the founder of Kingdom Shifters Ministries (KSM), Kingdom Shifters Empowerment Church, and Kingdom Wellness Counseling and Mentoring Center.

Credentials

Her expertise to undertake writing instructional books for ministry comes from the following:

- Doctorate in Theological Counseling and Ministry, Rapha Deliverance University
- Master of Science in Community Counseling – Emphasis on Marriage, Children, and Family Counseling, University of Missouri St. Louis
- Bachelor of Science in Psychology, Avila University
- Associate of Arts in Business Administration, Brown Mackie College
- Therapon Belief Therapist Certification, Therapon Institute
- Licensed in liturgical dance, Eagles Dance Institute with Dr. Pamela Hardy
- Ordination as Apostle, Jackie Green Ministries with Dr. Jackie Green
- Board member, New Day Community Ministries, Inc. with Dr. Kathy Williams

Dr. Baker is the author of 31 books and has recorded 2 CD's of prayer decrees.

Vision

Her expertise is built on many years of faithfully serving her local home church before launching Kingdom Shifters Ministries. At her previous church, she served as a prophet, overseer of the altar workers, and a member of the presbytery. She was used as a member of the Prophetic School team and as the visionary to launch the liturgical dance troupe Shekinah Expressions. She has served on multiple missions' trips to various Caribbean nations and has assisted with planting dance ministries in villages and cities throughout Haiti and Jamaica.

Dr. Baker is on a mission to expand the kingdom of God at every opportunity. She has been gifted in the following areas of expertise for helping likeminded kingdom citizens:

- Empowerment, assistance with launching ministries, businesses, and books;
- Mentoring, counseling, and releasing visions;
- Spiritual warfare, prayer, and administrating apostolic mandates;
- Establishing God's kingdom in individuals, ministries, communities, and regions.

Further, she is passionately committed to training others to understand and embrace destiny.

Please connect to Dr. Baker (Taquetta) through kingdomshifters.com or find her on Facebook.

TABLE OF CONTENTS

YOU ARE THE FIVEFOLD BLUEPRINT 1

RELIGIOUS DEPROGRAMMING 12

SHIFTING INTO A FIVEFOLD MINISTRY PARADIGM 21

VISION CASTING 26

CREATING MEASURABLE BLUEPRINT GOALS 49

BUILDING A FIVEFOLD MINISTRY TEAM 52

LEADERSHIP SOUL & VISION GOVERNING 56

FIVEFOLD MINISTRY TIER TEAMS 62

BUILDING A FIVEFOLD MINISTRY CULTURE 70

HEALTHY RELATIONSHIP NUGGETS 75

THE ART OF TRUE ACCOUNTABILITY 91

THE VALUE OF KINGDOM COVENANT 96

TRAINING & EQUIPPING 110

APOSTOLIC PROTOCOL 116

KINGDOM ARMORBEARORS 122

ADMINISTRATING FIVEFOLD MINISTRY 135

THE NECESSITY OF SUCCESSORS 146

DEMONIC HOOKS THAT KEEP YOU IN THE OLD 160

WARFARE & SUFFERINGS AS A VISION CARRIER 170

DRINKING THE FULL CUP OF DESTINY 174

BALANCING LIFE, DESTINY & THE VISION 185

SUGGESTIONS FOR TAKING RESPITE 191

BALANCING FAMILY & RELATIONSHIPS 197

FOREWORD

In my mid-30's, I had my first trip outside of the flatlands of the Midwest. The journey included Niagara Falls, the mountains of Vermont, and eventually the Atlantic Ocean. As I stood on top of Mt. Mansfield in Stowe, Vermont, tears ran down my face as I could only whisper, "Look how BIG God is!" When I saw the Atlantic Ocean for the first time, it replicated the mountain experience with the same level of breathtaking awe, "Look how BIG God is!" It also gave me a whole new respect for those that we historically reference as pioneers. What was in them that once they had crossed one mountain only to face another that they continued forward? What drove their quest for exploration that they did not falter through mountains and across rivers and deserts and more and more of the same? It is that same passion that drives certain leaders in the 21st-century church to leave their comfort zone and pursue greater vision. Dr. Taquetta Baker has a pioneering spirit that compels her to be restless until she has moved through every possibility with kingdom excellence. In this volume, she undertakes leaving the comfort of the traditional pastoral paradigm and walking through the journey of fivefold ministry. She takes time to set the stage by sharing her own struggles and challenges, mistakes and learning experiences so that the reader can have the advantages of learning from her pursuit of fivefold.

If you are a leader and reading this manual, Dr. Baker will serve as your co-pilot and guide through the intricacies of transition. If you are a member of a ministry, she is an invaluable traveling partner as you search whether God is persuading you toward the fivefold model. There is a principle called leadership-followership which is a relational interaction between those in each of the roles. As a member, you may be the follower with the assignment to nudge your leadership in embracing fivefold ministry. This volume is set in the tone of a journal so that you have opportunity to personalize each chapter with the concluding sets of questions. I encourage you to not only complete the questions but have an accountability partner or confidante that you can have conversations with about your responses. Dr. Baker brings substantiated expertise to this volume. She has a dynamic blend of professional and ministerial credentials that give strength to her voice as she calls out for those who are primed for fivefold ministry. Remember that pioneers are willing to press forward with no experience for what is ahead. It is that passionate drive that resulted in maps that allowed others to follow their path. This volume teaches you to become a fivefold trailblazer for the generations that will follow your footsteps.

Dr. Kathy E. Williams, Founder
New Day Community Ministries, Inc.

Foreword

In my nearly 50 years of team building, I find Volume Two refreshing and a wonderful blueprint for Kingdom teams. I call **Volume Two**, the Main Course of the three volumes. No vision can truly come forth without vision casting and teamwork. As I looked at this volume, I was reminded that my marriage of 46 years continues to be a vision casting and team building effort. Motherhood is a vision casting and team building effort. And finally, Ministry must be a team building and vision casting effort. I call these the **Three M"S**… Marriage, Motherhood and Ministry. Vision casting and team building is all around us in our everyday lives. For me I learned vision casting and team building in the Three M's.

But Dr. Baker specializes in Volume Two dealing with team building in ministry. She is very transparent about her own personal journey in ministry. She makes it clear that if we don't learn how to "**SHIFT**" throughout our ministry journeys, we will surely "**drift**" and never reach our full potential. Apostle Taquetta also spends extensive time explaining the clear role of the "vision carrier" and the tiers of leadership. I found the concept on the "Sojourner" or seasonal/inconsistent people in our churches and ministries are really "false vision carriers." They should be given tasks and minor responsibilities but not positions. To be able to identify such persons in our churches and ministries will save us a lot of hurts, disappointments and wasted time.

I felt that **Volume Two** takes us into deeper development of the fivefold operations with team building, vision casting, goal setting, accountability, conflict management, tools to train your teams and healthy communication skills. Dr. Baker spends ample time explaining the role of spiritual mothers and fathers. She says that" *Just because a person is your apostle, leader, etc., that does not automatically make them your spiritual parent. Spiritual mothers and fathers birth you. Mentors and leaders instruct and impart into you."*

I was really blessed by final sections of Volume Two dealing with the *"Necessity of Successors, Demonic Hooks and Bloodline Breakers."* These chapters are full of meat, not milk. The author shares: *"The problem today is that the church is so focused on the work and they have not properly positioned successors to carry on the work. They raised up disciples but not successors."* One of the demonic hooks that MOST ministries will deal with is Python, which keeps the Body of Christ in the old paradigms and squeeze the life and vision out of them. Her revelation on "breaking the head and the tail of the python" as it tries to wrap around the person, and the revelation that is flowing into that ministry and region is revelatory.

Volume Two delves into "**Bloodline Breakers**" which deal with the fact we must content against generational curses, cycles and patterns. The author shares from her own life experiences that:

> *"If you are called to be THE ONE in your family line to deal with these matters, then your destiny just became more complex as you are what I call the Kingdom Heir, also known as a Bloodline Breaker." Finally, the life instructions that one receives in*

Volume Two is not for beginners, but for those who desire strong meat and are ready to **SHIFT** from milk to meat, from vision complainers to vision carriers, from excuses to exploits, from just carrying the cup of destiny to drinking all that is in your cup, and from running themselves into the ground to resting in the Lord. **It is the main course.**

Dr. Baker could have concluded with Volume 2. We don't have to have desert with our meals. But thanks be to God, she wrote **Volume 3,** *the icing on the cake or the desert portion. Let's get ready to Shift to Volume 3.*

Shifting from Glory to Glory,
Bishop Dr Jackie L. Green-Apostle and Overseer
JGM International PrayerLife Institute, Redlands, CA

Endorsement

Apostolic leaders must constantly lean in for the downloads from heaven. It takes fresh manna to navigate the mandate. In this hour, God is raising up those apostolic pioneers who will move in power and authority, also teach, train and equip the people of God. Apostle Taquetta Baker is on the cutting edge. She has been in the ascended place receiving revelation and insight to release to you.

For who has known the mind of the Lord, that He will instruct him? But we have the mind of Christ. — 1 Corinthians 2:16

This manual unveils another dimension of the mind of God for Kingdom leaders and believers. It gives you tools and building blocks to fulfill Kingdom assignments. This is one of the gifts of an apostle. They steward the mysteries of God. They are entrusted with articulation for the Kingdom mandate. They speak to the depth of God locked deep inside the heart of man. They provide key words, key insights, and key nuggets to unblock mysteries. The mind of God is not locked away from us but ours to be discovered!

But we speak God's wisdom in a mystery, the hidden *wisdom* which God predestined before the ages to our glory;
the wisdom which none of the rulers of this age has understood; for if they had understood it they would not have crucified the Lord of glory; but just as it is written,
"Things which eye has not seen and ear has not heard,
And *which* have not entered the heart of man,
All that God has prepared for those who love Him." —1 Corinthians 2:7-9

As you read these pages, receive the wisdom of God. Receive answers and solutions. Receive strategies and plans. Receive direction and input. These words will prepare you for a greater level of function in the Kingdom of God!

Ryan LeStrange
Founder TRIBE/RLM/LeStrange Global LLC & iHubs
Author of Hell's Toxic Trio

YOU ARE THE FIVEFOLD BLUEPRINT

A blueprint is God's specific design for how we are to journey in destiny and produce his vision in the earth.

Even though my ministry has always been a fivefold paradigm and I was never fully indoctrinated into a pastoral paradigm, I spent twelve years laboring in a ministry that was striving to SHIFT from a pastoral to a fivefold paradigm. Fivefold seemed to just be a part of my identity as I found myself in provoking others to come into the fivefold mindset and lifestyle that the leaders had SHIFTED the ministry too. This was difficult because the leaders did not have a model for fivefold. They were learning and SHIFTING the ministry out of the religious and traditional setting as they themselves were learning to SHIFT out of it. One key that helped me navigate through this season was seeking God for where the ministry was in their transitional process from pastoral to fivefold and seeking God about what my role was in that process. I understood through seeking God that I had a part in them evolving. This required being bold and trusting what the Lord said to me as I continuously contended against religious and traditional spirits that were feisty and ruthless at times. I had to learn not to take the battle personal as the fight was not with the people. They were simply under the influence of what they had been taught and lived for years. My battle was with the principalities, territorial spirits, and powers that knew the greatness of the people within this ministry, the work God wanted to do through this ministry and in this region. It required continuous prayer, quickly forgiving, thick skin, knowing my identity and knowing many of their actions were not personal. They were learning and being broken free from these strongholds. It took years for freedom to occur and despite the persecution, it was worth the battle as the fruit of God's glory and kingdom advancement in my life, many of their lives, and within the ministry was evident.

I personally had to learn how to walk in fivefold ministry and practice not operating in a pastoral paradigm. I had to be delivered from what I knew about church, not succumb to what others believed church was, what others would consider to be comfortable regarding church, making sure bills were paid, etc. It has taken deliverance and education, especially since I did not have a blueprint or earthly role model to follow. I was my own unique fivefold blueprint. I had to trust my team and even receive feedback and constructive criticism when I was not operating in fivefold, but more of a pastoral model, and be open to constantly evaluating myself in this regard. I would also say that in my experience of helping others come out of a pastoral paradigm, character issues and fears of being replaced, losing control, relinquishing control, not being top dog, has been more of an issue than anything. Though there is still a leader in fivefold ministry, utilizing the team, and constantly creating teams is definitely the forefront of the paradigm. This requires teaching applicable tools of communication, conflict resolution, social and relational skills which most ministries do not do.

I was my own unique fivefold blueprint

When I started Kingdom Shifters Ministries (KSM), I had no clue I was building a true fivefold ministry. When I first launched it, I was a part of someone else's ministry. I was on their presbytery team, overseeing the altar workers ministry, the dance ministry, helping to teach Sunday School, prophetic school, launching conferences, training workshops, and whatever else God would grant to my hands. Though several years into laboring, I did know I was an apostle and many of my works revealed I was an apostle, I was recognized as a prophet. This was mostly because I was and still am adamant about having a word from the Lord. I was consistently giving a word, revelation, or strategy to help SHIFT and advance the ministry, the people, and the region. KSM was more of a dance and healing ministry at the time. I would travel abroad ministering in dance, while also helping to equip and establish dance ministries, deliverance teams, and altar workers ministries. I had begun mentoring people over the phone at 5am, but God did not reveal until later that I was building the Kingdom Wellness Counseling & Mentoring portion of my ministry.

When I transitioned out of the church to fully launch KSM, all God told me to do was to have a monthly Holy Ghost Agenda Service in my region. He did not say go build a fivefold ministry. I know some of you all are waiting on that word, but God is waiting on you to be obedient to the one thing he told you to do. HA! SHIFT RIGHT NOW! The vision of the service he told me to do was to provide monthly training and equipping in areas of fivefold ministry, while awakening revival reformation that would birth consistent miracles, signs, and wonders back into my region. I had no idea until later that this vision was the full mandate of my ministry. Aside from a lot of hands on experience and a dance ministry to which I had begun equipping the members in fivefold ministry and in their destiny - another mandate that was later revealed as another vision of KSM, I did not have any known insight to further launch my ministry.

All people saw me as was a dance ministry. Many gossiped and laughed at me saying - what does she think she going to do by leaving all of what she is doing now to further advance her "dance ministry." I did not have a clue what I was going to do. If I am honest with you, I felt like God was making me take a major SHIFT backwards though he claimed it to be a major leap forward. I would feel this way for years as my ministry was housed in my home where God hid, trained, and equipped my team and I. I felt exposed and vulnerable because I was used to having all the pieces to the puzzle and the full word of what God was telling me to do. This time, I only had in part and the part I had was not appearing very sturdy or glamorous. I felt embarrassed because I did not feel adequate or secure in what God was telling me to do and initially I had no one to help guide me. Some people, particularly leaders told me I would fail and was rebellious because they did not have vision for the SHIFT I was in. That was for somebody. You are waiting on others to validate your SHIFT. I am here to tell you that even some of those who prophesied who you would become, one day will be some of the same people who will curse your SHIFT because God did not enlighten their eyes to what he was doing in and through you in this new season. Their lack of sight will cause you to stay too long and even put you in the lion's den of unnecessary warfare, where you are actually being devoured because you are waiting on the "right" man - the one you want to hear from rather than the ones God already sent - to speak something God told you to do. But I digress.

God warned me that to remain where I was would be the detriment of me. I had finished that assignment and that book of my life had ended. Thus began a new book of destiny. If I did not SHIFT into the next series of my life, I would die at the end of that book. When I would explain this to people that were used to gleaning from who I was, all they could think about is what they were losing from the finished book of my identity. Most were angry with me for SHIFTING with God and ended their relationship with me. But none of them recognized what I would lose if I did not SHIFT with God. Many of them felt like I sacrificed them to do my own thing, but they sacrificed me because I did God's thing. So I must admit that some days I felt like the lonely worthless bad girl who everyone now hated because I could no longer be what they wanted or deemed valuable. The new value I had come into, most did not want or wanted to take advantage of it, because I was not publicly known enough for them to honor it like they did the big name platform preachers. But that is a whole other manual in and of itself. I shared all this to say that some of you are frustrated because you are at the end of a book of your destiny. A new series has started and you are waiting on God to give you more revelation before you are obedient to the few things he already told you to do. Some of you all are waiting on someone else to be the fivefold blueprint when you are the fivefold architect of your region. Some of you all are afraid to relinquish what you have already accomplished, especially since you are unsure what you will gain. I will say that with all I loss, and it was a lot. I loss mostly everything and everyone. I never felt so fulfilled in my life. There is nothing more comforting than being in the purpose of the Lord. And what I have gained is a continual evolving destiny accompanied with weighty revealed glory.

> **Romans 8:18** *For I reckon that the sufferings of this present time are not worthy to be compared with the glory which shall be revealed in us.*

As I SHIFTED with God, I learned that I was the blueprint for my fivefold ministry. A blueprint is God's specific design for how we are to journey in destiny and produce his vision in the earth. It embodies the fivefold ministry and pattern that I was looking for and wanting others to manifest. This was a hard pill to swallow, especially since I could gleam in measure from others, but had no true pioneers to blaze the trail that the Lord had me on. Many, I had encountered after I SHIFTED out of the church setting was still doing church but talking about fivefold, or only had a measure of fivefold operating in their ministry. It felt as if I was taking a step backwards or starting all over. But I learned quickly that I was not paving the way as blindly as I thought. The vision was in me. The vision was me. I was the blueprint.

> ***Psalms 139:14*** *I will praise you; for I am fearfully and wonderfully made: marvelous are your works; and that my soul knows right well.*
>
> ***New Living Translation*** *Thank you for making me so wonderfully complex! Your workmanship is marvelous – how well I know it.*

Knoweth is *yâḏa* in Hebrew. *Yada* is also a Hebrew word for praise. So, this knowing produces and even is a praise that we are to have about who we are in God.

<u>*Yada* in Hebrew means:</u>
1. to know and ascertain by seeing
2. to know by observation, care, recognition
3. to know causatively, by instruction, by designation, and even by punishment (so there is some life lessons and experiences that SHIFTS your soul into revelation of who you are versus who you are not)
4. to acknowledge, to come into acquaintance, to be advised, to receive answers about, to appoint
5. to assuredly know, be aware of
6. to certainly know, to comprehend, to consider, to be cunning in your knowing

- ❖ Your soul knows such that it declares it; it can diligently discern, and even help you discover who you are.
- ❖ Your soul is endued with a knowing of who you are; it is like a familiar friend, it is famous for revealing the truth of you.
- ❖ It is designed to instruct you regarding the truth of your identity and does just that, it is like kinsfolk, kinsman, that can speak on your behalf.

There is a clear innate understanding within our souls about the uniqueness and wonderfulness to which we were created and who we are. The only way to not discern our true identity blueprint is to reject it or refuse to acknowledge it. But it has been put in the DNA of our souls to know who we are, to boast of who we are, and to evolve into who we are in the earth.

This is the reason I was able to operate in fivefold ministry at my previous church and be successful. I possessed the DNA for my destiny and calling within me. I was destined to release the blueprint God had placed in me before the foundation of the earth, so even as I SHIFTED into my own ministry, I was able to trust God for the part of the vision he was giving me. Then as I was obedient, my fivefold ministry blueprint evolved from within me.

This is the reason the disciples were able to put down their nets and follow Jesus. It was in them already to SHIFT to a daily lifestyle with him and to be fishers of men. And even as each of them followed Jesus and he taught them collectively about fishing for lives, their apostleship manifested in a different and unique way according to the unique identity blueprint of God that was within them. You see,

- ✓ Each fivefold ministry blueprint is distinct and tailor made to our identity.
- ✓ Each fivefold ministry blueprint also begins with us – Jesus being the chief cornerstone.
- ✓ Each fivefold ministry blueprint has a standard and as God works his standard in us, the fivefold ministry blueprint begins to manifest in us, through us as we release glimpses of it in our daily interactions and opportunities, and outside of us as we begin to clearly understand the vision and seek to fully establish it in the earth.

Matthew 16:17-18 And Jesus answered and said unto him, Blessed art thou, Simon Barjona: for flesh and blood hath not revealed it unto thee, but my Father which is in heaven. And I say also unto thee, That thou art Peter, and upon this rock I will build my church; and the gates of hell shall not prevail against it.

Ephesians 2:19-22 Now, therefore, you are no longer strangers and foreigners, but fellow citizens with the saints and members of the household of God, having been built on the foundation of the apostles and prophets, Jesus Christ Himself being the chief cornerstone, in whom the whole building, being fitted together, grows into a holy temple in the Lord, in whom you also are being built together for a dwelling place of God in the Spirit.

One of the foundational truths religious doctrine took from the body of Christ was the ability to SHIFT into our unique fivefold ministry blueprints. In effort to bring order, instill clear biblical lifestyle applications, and have a specific design that keeps people from idolatry, mixture and being tossed to and fro, man created doctrinal systems. The systems became ministry blueprints that people patterned their identity blueprints after, rather than after the unique design of destiny that God put in them. This is the reason many ministers have challenges trying to find balance between the doctrinal systems they have submitted to and the unique ministry blueprint that is trapped within their souls.

Biblically, religious doctrines was to teach us the nature, character and standards of God. It was never to create religious systems (e.g. Baptists, Methodists, Pentecostal, Nondenominational) that separated us into religious sects and have us fighting over who is really doing it God's way.

> **2Timothy 3:16-17** *All scripture is given by inspiration of God, and is profitable for doctrine, for reproof, for correction, for instruction in righteousness: That the man of God may be perfect, throughly furnished unto all good works.*

I believe one of the reasons Jesus visited the apostles after his resurrection was to allow them to personally see that his identity blueprint was fulfilled, but also further awaken their unique identity blueprint for advancing the gospel within them. Up to this point, they had operated as a group of disciples and apostles who loved Jesus, but had not grasped that they were being specifically equipped and released for official fivefold ministry military service. Witnessing the full blueprint of Jesus, provided personal clarity for all they had been told would happen regarding Jesus, and taught and equipped to do regarding ministry.

- Jesus privately appearing to Peter and assuring him he had risen – ***Luke 24:34***
- Jesus then appearing to Peter and telling him to feed his sheep – ***John 21:17***
- Jesus appearing to Cleopas and another disciple while they were on the road to Emmaus – ***Luke 24:13-19***
- Jesus appearing to the disciples (Thomas was absent) on Easter Sunday – ***John 20:19, 20, 24***
- Jesus appearing to the disciples again (Thomas was present) – ***John 20:26-28***

- ❖ Jesus appearing to seven disciples at the Sea of Galilee – *John 21:1-2*
- ❖ Jesus appearing o eleven disciples at the mountain of Galilee – *Matthew 28:16-17*
- ❖ After his ascension, Jesus appeared again to Saul of Tarsus who became Paul on the road to Damascus – *Acts 9:3-5*

These appearances SHIFTED them into the full reality and accountability of what their soul already knew about them and what Jesus continuously poured into them.

Can you imagine:
- ❖ In your zeal of putting down your nets to follow Jesus?
- ❖ Journeying with Jesus in tangible covenant relationship?
- ❖ Watching, experiencing, and doing great wonders with Jesus?
- ❖ Getting to sit at his feet and be personally taught and spiritually fed?
- ❖ Jesus telling you he is going to die and resurrect and you hearing these stories growing up but never grasping the fullness of them?
- ❖ Thinking you are with Jesus because it seemed cool at the time, but then BAMM!!! Every soul unction you had, every decision you made, every experience you had, finally begins to make sense?
- ❖ That your life was not just a thrilling ride unfolding?
- ❖ You were in destiny?
- ❖ You were in the peak of your calling and there was more of you to evolve as you further activated what was already in you and what was imparted to train you for what was already in you????

WOWWWWW! SHIFT RIGHT NOW! SHIFT!

What happened to the apostolic disciples is what happens too many of us who awaken in our fivefold ministry calling.

I always tell people I was tricked into ministry. Even though I was raised in church, drug to church, and as a sinner still went to church, studied my bible, and consistently prayed, I never knew I was a going to be a minister, book writer, kingdom heir, pioneer, trailblazer, Kingdom SHIFTER, apostle, gatekeeper, creator of kingdom paradigms and the list just keeps unfolding.

- I just loved Jesus.
- Then I just wanted to live for Jesus.

- Then Jesus sent me a spiritual mother. I just wanted to be with her and be obedient to the word I received about walking in ministry with her for a season, so I resisted going to Texas where I always wanted to live, and moved from Illinois to Indiana.
- Even in its challenges, I just wanted to please God, so I was obedient and sold out to him.
- And then all of these other parts of my life that my soul knew that I did not know began to unfold.

I would say that even though I had 12 years of preparation with Jesus, my resurrection encounter came when God told me it was time to leave my church and SHIFT into my own ministry. Like the disciples,

- I continued to receive hands on Holy Spirit training.
- I would release that training every opportunity I got and God created opportunities for me to be continuously used.
- I would study books, sermons, tapes, and teachings as the Holy Spirit led me.
- I would travel and attend conferences, prophetic, deliverance, healing, evangelist, dance ministry schools and trainings, and then return to my church and impart and train others in what I learned.
- I would pioneer works within and outside the ministry as the Holy Spirit led.
- I would ignite church after church services because the presence of the Lord was so tangible in the ministry I was attending and so I would pursue miracles, signs, and wonders. I would train the altar workers in the gifts of the spirit and to pursue manifestation. So after church I would still be praying and giving people words which caused them to flow in this as well. God would move and we would be worshiping and praising him and folks were delivered, healed, filled with the Holy Spirit, seeking to be baptized, etc.

I was always where the Holy Ghost party was or starting one. I was a kingdom SHIFTER and even as I named my ministry Kingdom Shifters Ministries, I did not have my resurrection moment until I realized that all of what I had been doing was for the full vision that was about to unfold in my own personal ministry. I was the blueprint of fivefold ministry. I was what I was trying to make everybody else be. And everyone was not going to be like me because they too possessed their own unique fivefold ministry blueprint that needed to be released in the earth.

Even as I consider my process with the Holy Spirit and think of all the people I have come across that have said, "the Holy Spirit taught me what I know about my identity, calling and fivefold ministry," I am reminded of these scriptures:

> *John 14:26* *But the Comforter, which is the Holy Ghost, whom the Father will send in my name, he shall teach you all things, and bring all things to your remembrance, whatsoever I have said unto you.*
>
> *John 15:26* *When the Advocate comes, whom I will send to you from the Father--the Spirit of truth who goes out from the Father--He will testify about Me.*
>
> *John 16:13* *However, when the Spirit of truth comes, He will guide you into all truth. For He will not speak on His own, but He will speak what He hears, and He will declare to you what is to come.*
>
> *1Corinthians 2:10* *But God has revealed it to us by the Spirit. The Spirit searches all things, even the deep things of God.*

MY GOD! When we accept Jesus Christ as our personal savior and the Holy Spirit enters our vessels, our communion with him helps guide us into the truth of what our souls already house regarding our identity. Some of you are challenged that you have only had the Holy Spirit to teach you; even to the point of being offended with those who could not speak into your lives and train you. Even to the point of being angry with God that no one has really been able to speak into who you are or train you. But this is the Holy Spirit's mandate in our lives. And as we evolve in identity, God will send those we need along the way. However, we first must come into a PEACE and embrace in knowing that we are the blueprint.

These fivefold ministry manuals are written to help you realize that you are the blueprint and to help you awaken the unique identity blueprint that is on the inside of you. YOU MUST COME FORTH! YOU MUST SHIFT FORTH!

- ❖ The body of Christ awaits you.

- ❖ The world awaits you.
- ❖ The marketplace awaits you.
- ❖ The community and region awaits you.
- ❖ Your remnant and the people that need you awaits you.
- ❖ Your soul is awaiting to boast of God through what will evolve through you.

I DECREE A SHIFT INTO YOU TODAY TO ACCEPT THAT YOU ARE GOD'S UNIQUE FIVEFOLD MINISTRY BLUEPRINT! SHIFT!

Homework Explorations:
1. Journal in detail your thoughts on this chapter.
2. Ask God what part of your book of life are you in. Journal what he speaks.
3. What has God told you to do that you have not done yet?
4. What is your biggest fear with stepping out in what the Lord has spoken to you.
5. What do you think you need before being obedient to what God has said? Ask God if these are necessities to doing what he has said? Journal what he says. If he says they are not, then go forth. If he says they are then align yourself with him for those necessities to be released to you.
6. Spend time soaking your soul in the glory of God. Journal regarding the unctions your soul has already given you over the course of your life and the ones you are receiving as you are consumed by the glory of God.
7. Share how Holy Spirit has journeyed with you in teaching you what you know about Jesus, your identity, your calling, and about fivefold ministry.
8. Ask God whether you are the fivefold blueprint that you keep seeking. Journal what he reveals.
9. SHIFT RIGHT NOW! SHIFT AGAIN!

RELIGIOUS DEPROGRAMMING

Deprogramming entails the releasing of someone from apparent brainwashing, typically that of a religious organization, a cult, culture and traditional ideologies or mindsets, political indoctrinations, by the systematic reindoctrination of conventional values. With deprogramming, the leader and vision carriers will have to consistently re-educate themselves and the members regarding God, their identity, destiny, calling, sound doctrine, and fivefold ministry, to dismantle religious doctrines, religious and traditional behaviors and ideologies, boxed in methodologies about God, and what living for God really means and looks like. This will require replacing learned or acquired behavior patterns, habits, and perceptions that are undesirable or unsuitable, with a new daily lifestyle covenant with God, sound doctrine, and the New Testament fivefold vision that God provides.

Deprograming is one of the most vital yet sensitive processes to SHIFTING from a traditional church paradigm to a fivefold ministry paradigm. The person will have to relinquish what they think they know about God, themselves, and ministry, for the sake of learning church and kingdom from a whole new perspective. It is not that what they knew is not valuable. They will recognize how intricate all of it truly is as they SHIFT with God. But it will take the process to assist them with completely relinquishing what God contends is not beneficial to their new fivefold ministry paradigm.

I equate deprograming to closing a book of life regarding one's journey with God and opening a whole other book that has not been written yet. The new book is written by walking out this new pathway of evolving destiny with God. Since a book was closed and not a chapter, it is not a continuation of a season or lifespan, but a SHIFTING into a new era of one's destiny and calling with God. When this is not realized or actualized, the transition can become confusing and frustrating. The deprograming process can be challenging because of,

- The continual re-education and education of the new vision and how the person and their relationship with God impacts the vision.
- Being corrected when they yield to traditional church mentalities and behaviors that hinder rather than bless their progress and process.

- Having to work the process and resist getting ahead of God and the momentum of laying a solid foundation for the vision.
- Trusting the main vision carrier and the new way he or she leads versus a traditional church leader.
- Battling through the psychological lies of spiritual warfare that the enemy will send to abort their progress and process. Principalities and territorial spirits will send fears, lies, misperceptions, in effort to get people to mistrust the leader and the vision, where they abort their transition with God and the reason he made them a part of the vision.
- Outside familiar influences that do not understand a true fivefold paradigm having a negative impact on those who are a part of it. These familiar influences plant seeds of suspicion, doubt, and fear that make it difficult for the person to feel secure in the SHIFT God is doing in their lives. Their need for love and belonging will cause them to feel torn between the familiar and what they are building with those in the fivefold vision.

Some people who have church hurt, unresolved soul wounds, or mistrust issues will have difficulty with being deprogrammed. They will require patience and support. It would be beneficial to provide a mentor or cell group to assist them with the process. They will have lots of questions and emotional anxieties that will need to be worked out.

The most difficult people to deprogram are those who have been saved a long time and/or have already been used in ministry. There are also those who have a strong desire to be used and are excited about fivefold ministry. They take what little revelation they have been taught or the freedom that comes with fivefold to justify their perceived readiness to be utilized in ministry NOW, even though they still need training and a reprogramming. Many people in these categories will succumb to pride. They will begin to boast about what they already know and have accomplished with God. They will want special considerations, and definitely should be given some based on their maturity, loyalty to God and his kingdom, and expertise. The challenge will be encouraging them to adhere to the process of deprograming and the laying of a solid fivefold foundation, so they can be released successfully, and in God's timing regarding the vision. If pride breeds impatience, they may begin usurping authority and sowing discord, making negative inferences and false accusations against leadership and the ministry, or leave the ministry altogether. Often, the main leader will want to initially place these members as vision carriers, particularly because God will choose them due to their faithfulness. But please know some of them may abort. They will be God chosen but pride will destroy their chance. It is just a part of how the vision exposes what is not of God and what cannot be rooted in the foundation of the vision. It occurred with Judas, and thus may occur as you plant your fivefold ministry. Sigh!!!

No one is beyond needing to be deprogrammed, not even the major vision carrier/s. All will have to succumb to this process. Even the disciples were deprogrammed. They were not aware that it was occurring, but their entire journey with Jesus as he walked the earth, was a deprogramming of the old paradigm into the new. The Samaritan woman was deprogrammed. She fully recognized it and was able to SHIFT into evangelizing a region because she surrendered to the reconstitution of spiritual reformation during her encounter with Jesus.

In John 4 (Study the chapter), we have Jesus engaging the Samaritan woman at the well of Jacob in the region of Samaria. Samaritans were half Jew and half Gentile. Their race derived from being held in captivity by Assyrians. Once freed, some of the Jews stayed behind and intermarried. Jacob's well served as a religious altar of worship unto God for them, while the pure Jewish race worshiped on the mountain in Jerusalem. The Samaritans had their own temple and replica of the Torah. This was the reason these two groups of people had conflicts with one another. The pure Jews did not like that they engaged in interracial activities and had their own worship site and rituals. Sound like us today huh? SHIFT RIGHT NOW!

Jesus asked the woman for a drink. She immediately acknowledged their cultural, racial, and religious contentions by saying, "you ask me for a drink, the Jews have no dealings with Samaritans." Jesus sparked the woman's curiosity by saying that being able to serve him water was a big deal because of who he was. He was the living water. The woman told Jesus that he had nothing to draw with but still inquired about the living water. The woman then began to inquire whether Jesus was greater than the religious and traditional doctrines and ideologies she knew about regarding Jacob's well, her ancestors and God. Jesus let her know that indeed he was and was the savior they spoke of and worshiped. He did this by expressing that if she drank of his water that it shall be in her a well of water springing up into everlasting life. The lady immediately wanted some of Jesus' water. She willingly was open to giving up the old water and even the natural water, for his new everlasting water.

Jesus further deprogrammed the woman by asking her to go get her husband and then he would give her some of his water. Jesus had deprogrammed her spirit, now he was deprogramming her soul. MY GOD! The lady said I have no husband. Jesus prophetically began to speak truth to her by the knowledge of God. He expressed that he knew she was husband less, that she had already had five husbands, and the man she was with now was just a boyfriend. The Samaritan woman recognized Jesus' prophetic edge and SHIFTED into what she knew about being spiritual. This is what we tend to do when God is coming for our old paradigm, we try to use it to show that we are familiar with him - that we already know things about him and his kingdom - that we already know about worshipping and serving him. But that is our soul speaking, which is understandable because once our soul encounters Jesus, it cannot un-know it. This is the reason God says in Roman 1 that when we begin to worship created idols and do not heed his warnings, that he turns us over to a reprobate mind. Once we hear of Jesus, we can deny him, but we can never un-know him.

Deprograming is one of the most vital yet sensitive processes to SHIFTING from a traditional church paradigm to a fivefold ministry paradigm.

Romans 1:18-26 *For the wrath of God is revealed from heaven against all ungodliness and unrighteousness of men, who hold the truth in unrighteousness; Because that which may be known of God is manifest in them; for God hath shewed it unto them. For the invisible things of him from the creation of the world are clearly seen, being understood by the things that are made, even his eternal power and Godhead; so that they are without excuse: Because that, when they knew God, they glorified him not as God, neither were thankful; but became vain in their imaginations, and their foolish heart was darkened. Professing themselves to be wise, they became fools, And changed the glory of the uncorruptible God into an image made like to corruptible man, and to birds, and fourfooted beasts, and creeping things. Wherefore God also gave them up to uncleanness through the lusts of their own hearts, to dishonour their own*

> *bodies be hearts, to dishonour their own bodies between themselves: Who changed the truth of God into a lie, and worshipped and served the creature more than the Creator, who is blessed for ever. Amen. For this cause God gave them up unto vile affections: for even their women did change the natural use into that which is against nature.*

I threw that revelation in for free - back to deprograming. Jesus was not asking her to un-know what she had learned, but to expand her mind and lifestyle to a new way of knowing him. And to allow him to show her what about the old could SHIFT into this new paradigm with him. Jesus knew that he was about to die and be raised to throne room living. He was about to close a book. A new era of covenant and destiny living was about to be unveiled. He needed her soul to align with the spiritual SHIFT that had already taken place when she asked for his living water.

When the woman began to proudly - pridefully - share her religious revelation on the doctrine of worship, Jesus said, "Woman, believe me, the hour cometh, when ye shall neither in this mountain, nor yet at Jerusalem, worship the Father. Ye worship ye know not what: we know what we worship: for salvation is of the Jews. But the hour cometh, and now is, when the true worshippers shall worship the Father in spirit and in truth: for the Father seeketh such to worship him. God is a Spirit: and they that worship him must worship him in spirit and in truth. (John 4:26)." Whewwww! The woman was being SHIFTED into understanding that worship is not:

- ❖ A place
- ❖ A building
- ❖ A certain location or destination
- ❖ A certain time
- ❖ A certain time zone
- ❖ A certain season or festivity
- ❖ A certain movement or expression
- ❖ An emotion or emotional activity
- ❖ A replication of what others do just to say they do it
- ❖ An act that lacks understanding, relationship and connection
- ❖ A religious act just because your ancestors or culture do it

> ***Verse 21-24 The Amplified Bible*** *Jesus said to her, Woman, believe Me, a time is coming when you will worship the Father neither [merely] in this mountain nor [merely] in Jerusalem. You [Samaritans] do not know what*

you are worshiping [you worship what you do not comprehend]. We do know what we are worshiping [we worship what we have knowledge of and understand], for [after all] salvation comes from [among] the Jews. A time will come, however, indeed it is already here, when the true (genuine) worshipers will worship the Father in spirit and in truth (reality); for the Father is seeking just such people as these as His worshipers. God is a Spirit (a spiritual Being) and those who worship Him must worship Him in spirit and in truth (reality).

Jesus SHIFTED the Samaritan woman into understanding that worship was a daily lifestyle of spirit to spirit covenant relationship with God. The woman further expressed that she knew the Messiah was coming to tell her about herself and save her. Jesus let the woman know that she was talking to her Messiah - she was drinking living water. The woman left her water jar and went into town telling everyone to come see her Messiah and drink of his living water. Leaving her water jar was symbolic of leaving the religious paradigm and even the tradition cultural and racial hatred behind, and SHIFTING into the new. She did not even allow the marveling of the disciples who returned and were puzzled at her and Jesus communing sway her. She closed a book of life and SHIFTED into a new one. Her new life entailed a SHIFT from just doing works to operating in her calling. From just living a life hearing about Jesus to personally encountering being transformed by Jesus. From just accepting what her culture and ancestors conditioned her life to be regarding worship, to saving a region with her free proclamation of worship.

> *John 4:28-30 Then the woman left her water jar and went away to the town. And she began telling the people, Come, see a Man Who has told me everything that I ever did! Can this be [is not this] the Christ? [Must not this be the Messiah, the Anointed One?] So the people left the town and set out to go to Him.*

The Samaritan woman did not allow the old, suspicions, doubts, or fears get in the way of her SHIFT and neither should you. God is deprograming you because he has better living water for you that shall spring up within you life everlasting. He is not trying to take from you, control you, or hurt you. He wants to evolve your life all the more where your lifestyle is worship unto him, and where true spirit to spirit encounters is your daily portion with him.

Being deprogrammed is not a cultish act. I want to dismantle this myth because it is a major accusation that derives when SHIFTING from a pastoral to a fivefold paradigm. I am not saying some leaders have not displayed controlling or cultish behavior, but all fivefold ministries are not bad or cults just like traditional churches are not controlling or cults. Fivefold ministry SHIFTS you to spirit to spirit worship which is not what many of us have been taught to do, so God is going to come for what will get in the way of this SHIFT. He will come for it personally and will instruct our leaders to deprogram it. Our soul and flesh will not like it. Sometimes we will not understand it. Sometimes it will feel like punishment or chastisement. Sometimes it will feel embarrassing and exposing. Jesus told the woman she had five husbands and a new boyfriend. That could not have felt good. But when we consider what true spirit to spirit worship is, we recognize that our total being and life is being offered up as a sacrifice of worship. All of who we are is being sacrificed every day all day to God.

> **Romans 8:36** *As it is written, For thy sake we are killed all the day long; we are accounted as sheep for the slaughter.*

When we do not embrace the deprogramming we can feel the cuts of being sacrificed, but when we accept it as a necessary lifestyle, we no longer feel the cutting. For we are not focused on what God is cutting away. We are focused on who we are becoming.

Deprogramming takes total humility. The Samaritan woman did not justify her sin, make excuses for her sin, or hide her sin. She did change the subject and become religious. HA! But she eventually SHIFTED to total humility which caused her transformation.

> **Psalms 51:17** *The sacrifices of God are a broken spirit: a broken and a contrite heart, O God, thou wilt not despise.*

<u>*Sacrifices* is *zebah* in Hebrew and means:</u>
1. properly, a slaughter, i.e. the flesh of an animal
2. by implication, a sacrifice (the victim or the act)
3. offer(-ing), sacrifice, offer, thank offering

<u>*Broken* is *săbar* in Hebrew and means:</u>
1. to burst (literally or figuratively)

2. break (down, off, in pieces, up), broken((-hearted)), bring to the birth, crush, destroy, hurt, quench, quite, tear, view, break in pieces, hurt, torn, give birth, crush, quench
3. rend violently, wreck, crush, quench, to rupture to be broken, be maimed, be crippled, be wrecked, to shatter

<u>Contrite is *daka*ˆ in Hebrew and means:</u>
1. to collapse (phys. or mentally): — break (sore), contrite, crouch.
2. to crush, be crushed, be contrite, be broken, to be crushed, collapse, to crush down, to crush to pieces

<u>Despise is *bâza*ˆ in Hebrew and means:</u>
1. to disesteem, despise, disdain
2. contemptible, to scorn, to be a vile person

The only way we become a genuine sacrifice is to totally humble ourselves, and true humility entails a crushing, a breaking, and a total collapsing in the Lord. I remember getting a prophecy that God was going to use me so mightily in the days to come that I would have to fall out the chariot daily as an act of humility and worship unto God. Upon being given this word, I immediately had a vision of that very thing occurring. I asked the Holy Spirit to never take that vision away and it has become my continual conviction. I see it or I am reminded of it constantly. Especially when I feel justified to gloat about something, or when I sense God avenging me or blessing me in front of my enemies. It always pops up to remind me to stay pure, meek, and humble. Sometimes I pray and worship with that vision in mind. I am just falling out of the chariot and offering praises and worship to God. It has helped me live self-sacrificing. Where I willingly sacrifice myself and have no other desire but to please God. This is the dimension of deprogramming I want to forever live in and decree it is your portion. God has some spectacular things ahead for you. I decree you fall out of the chariot of the old paradigm, and live eternally prostrated in your daily destiny being a lifestyle of spirit to spirit fivefold worship with Jesus. SHIFT!

In addition to falling out of the chariot, another weapon for deprogramming is the use of the battering ram.

<u>Britannica.com defines a *battering rams* as:</u> "Battering ram, ancient and medieval weapon consisting of a heavy timber, typically with a metal knob or point at the front. Such devices were used to batter down the

gates or walls of a besieged city or castle. The ram itself, usually suspended by ropes from the roof of a movable shed, was swung back and forth by its operators against the besieged structure. The roof of the shed was usually covered with animal skins to protect the weapon's operators from bombardment with stones or fiery materials."

> ***Micah 2:13*** *The breaker goes up before them; They break out, pass through the gate and go out by it. So their king goes on before them, And the LORD at their head."*

The battering ram will have to be utilized to pull down and demolish demonic structures within one's own life, generational line, people, the church, ministries, visions and blueprints, regions and spheres. Religion, tradition, demonic structures and strongholds, generational cultures and ideologies, ungodly or unhealthy beliefs, ancient fortified walls, gates, and fortresses, will have to be battered in prayer and by living the destiny lifestyle that God is SHIFTING the person and vision into. Battering ram prayers and actions breaks down anything down that hinders access to what God is saying or doing. The battering can be the use of repetitious words, scriptures, decrees, lyrics, sounds, movements, laws, standards, promises, prophecies, actions, behaviors, activities, to dismantle and crumble a blockage or stronghold. The premise is to persistently pound, hammer, beat, blast, damage, wreck, weaken, killing the target repeatedly until it yields way continual lifestyle of daily destiny and fivefold vision. I DECREE that you embody the weapon of a battering ram, such that you are deprogrammed from anything that deprives you from the true liberty of all God desires and has for you. SHIFT RIGHT NOW! SHIFT!

Homework Explorations:
1. Journal your thoughts on this chapter. Specifically share regarding the process of the woman at the well.
2. Why is deprogramming essential to one's fivefold journey?
3. Search pride areas and propensities in you with God. Journal what he reveals to you.
4. Journal your thoughts on being a sacrifice, broken, contrite, and despised.
5. What areas of your life need to be truly SHIFTED where you enter into true humility of being a daily sacrifice unto the Lord?

SHIFTING INTO A FIVEFOLD MINISTRY PARADIGM

SEEKING GOD FOR FIVEFOLD VISION

Fivefold ministry is more than just free worship, praying and prophesying to one another, experiencing some deliverance and healing, yet still living in a measure of salvation. After you fall out in the glory and get back up, there should be evident transformation, impartation and hunger to live for, build up, release, establish, and advance the kingdom of God in the earth. Let me provide some applicable keys of how to SHIFT into fivefold ministry.

- ✓ Seek God for a fivefold ministry vision. Seek him for what part of the vision is to be released first. Begin releasing that part and only release and evolve other portions of the vision at his leading.
- ✓ Study and train on what the fivefold ministry is; learn and teach the gifts and operations continually.
- ✓ SHIFT to studying and utilizing more scriptural references of the apostolic and the prophetic. This will help create a new fivefold ministry culture, climate and lingo that will further activate the fivefold in your midst.
- ✓ Identify vision carriers, team members and partners. Add and take away as God leads. Be okay that some may start with you but may decide not to be apart as the new vision unfolds. SHIFT into consciously recognizing that as the leader, you do not have to carry the ministry alone. The leader will always embody more of the weight of the vision, but it is a team vision so the weight is also shared with the other vision carriers and team members. The team members should take ownership and responsibility for carrying their share of the vision. As they are identified, they should seek God for their purpose as vision carriers and team members. The leader should be able to confirm what God is saying to them. They should have clear distinct understanding that their position within the ministry is a God ordained part of their destiny and they should be able to articulate that and demonstrate it as they help to carry and release the ministry vision.
- ✓ Practice SHIFTING to a complete mindset of teamwork and providing platforms and opportunities for each person that is a part of the team - the vision carriers - to come forth.

- ✓ Learn each vision carriers' unique destiny, calling, and identity. Seek ways to cultivate and SHIFT them in this as a lifestyle. Learn the same regarding team members, partners, and members as a whole.
- ✓ Assist vision carriers and team members with releasing their own personal unique destiny blueprints. This is what helps with evolving and advancing the ministry vision and the kingdom and awakening revival reformation in the community and region. The more members are operating in destiny, the greater the kingdom has come into your midst. And the more the ministry is able to infiltrate, overtake, and displace worldly systems.
- ✓ Include the vision carriers in the decision making regarding the ministry vision, ministry opportunities, trainings and events, ministry SHIFTS, directions, team members and partners, prayer and vision strategies, vision goals, financial endeavors, etc.
- ✓ Provide vision carriers and team members room and grace to grow. As tasks are delegated, do not lord over them. Give them deadlines to complete what they need to do for the ministry and in their destiny endeavors. This will aid them in learning to be accountable vision carriers and team members. Provide constructive criticism and feedback as needed to promote growth and consistency with being responsible vision carriers and team members. Be realistic regarding what may not be a strength and where duties may need to be reassigned if it appears to be a continual challenge for that person to fulfill. Provide more conducive assignments that are in alignment with that person's strengths, destiny, and calling.
- ✓ SHIFT to making sure leaders and vision carriers are assessable, while also delegating duties properly where they are not unnecessarily drained by challenges that could be handled by capable team members.
- ✓ SHIFT the members from just receiving and being encouraged through the ministry to engaging in personal destiny.
- ✓ Create ministry and educational tracks for licensing and ordination so that members and partners can be trained, equipped and released in their destiny and calling.
- ✓ Provide ongoing training and equipping for the building up of the ministry, edification of the saints, strengthening of faith and relationship with God, destiny attainment and revival reformation.
- ✓ SHIFT to teaching all members how to live a daily lifestyle with God not just during weekly gatherings.
- ✓ SHIFT to building a vision that is beyond Sunday services and church programs. Revival reformation is not just glory services but making a

consistent kingdom impact in the earth outside the four walls of the church.
- ✓ Practice being futuristic in your thinking, planting, building, and advancing such that the vision is focused on flourishing throughout generations.
- ✓ Position successors; train and equip them to carry the vision from generation to generation.
- ✓ Train and equip children and teens in their destiny and callings so they can live for God and through their ordained purpose in the earth. This is also essential for revival reformation and positioning successors to carry the ministry legacy throughout generations.
- ✓ SHIFT to being vulnerable where God can deprogram and reprogram each member from the leader on down to every member. This is essential where there may have been years of operating in the pastoral paradigm or not knowing what fivefold ministry is. Doctrines and ideologies have to be rooted out of the heart, mind, soul, and behaviors of each person individually, families, and the ministry culture. Be at peace about revisiting the foundation even if you have been building for years and have successful fruit. It may be essential to uproot parts of the pastoral foundation or do away with the foundation all together and start afresh.
- ✓ Some people may not be on board with building God's way as the SHIFT into a fivefold ministry paradigm occurs. They may leave. Be okay with the pruning that may occur before new growth occurs.
- ✓ SHIFT to shared mic ministry. Each vision carrier and team member should be given opportunity to be utilized during services and events as God leads. This promotes healthy identity and ministry growth, and team ministry where the gifts and callings are flowing freely and consistently. Share the duties of preaching, praying, prophesying, teaching and casting out devils. This is the foundation and strength of fivefold ministry.
- ✓ Promote a culture that ministry is in the market place, educational system, media and entertainment, politics and economics, community, etc., so that those who are called to these arenas can take their rightful place and know that they are just as valuable as those who may engage in mic ministry. Create opportunities for them to be trained and equipped to minister in these settings. Even allow the unbelievers to help train and equip where necessary.
- ✓ SHIFT into honoring and making sure the people know it is ok for them to be different and to be cultivated in their own unique identity. It is important for each person to genuinely be themselves because

who they truly are in God is what is needed in the ministry. Carbon copies will not be useful. We need puzzle pieces to fit, not be stacked on top of one another. We need each individual piece to operate in fullness. The culture and environment of the ministry and households should be one where each person knows, feels, and experiences that they can be comfortable in both discovering, expressing and operating in who they uniquely are in God. Each person should be respected, honored, trained and equipped in that uniqueness.
- ✓ SHIFT to living and flowing with the agenda, momentum, guidance, and flow of the Holy Spirit and being open to changes in services, events and programs as the Holy Spirit leads.
- ✓ SHIFT in your mindset regarding your fivefold ministry. One office is not "more powerful" or "better" than the other. A great way to think about the fivefold is if you were to make a fist with your hand. It takes ALL of the offices to work together and one is not standing taller than the other.
- ✓ It will be essential to dismantle the spirit of religion and tradition. Everyone must be empowered in the liberty of the Holy Spirit and in their relationship with God where they live by and through the personal standards he gives them for godly living. This becomes the order and doctrine for their lives as they also learn to honor and be governed by the laws, standards and apostolic order God provides in releasing the ministry vision.
- ✓ Implement God's examples and blueprints of ministry, fellowship, building, empowerment, preaching, and teaching found in the New Testament.
- ✓ SHIFT to teaching, understanding, and activating the concept of covenant and being accountable to each other.
- ✓ SHIFT from master slave mentalities in all areas. Create a culture of healthy dialogue and interaction, by teaching and practicing applicable healthy communication skills, conflict resolution skills, social skills, interpersonal skills, and healthy family and relationship skills.
- ✓ Cultivate a culture and climate of love and healthy fellowship where honor and servanthood is present and active in leadership, consistently demonstrated for the members to bestow one to another, and role model as people are added to the ministry.
- ✓ SHIFT from the poverty Jesus was poor so we should be poor mindset to acceptance of prosperity and blessing of God as a kingdom heirs.

Homework Explorations:

1. Journal five significant keys you learned from this chapter that will be important to your fivefold ministry blueprint.
2. Journal five significant differences you recognize between a pastoral paradigm and a fivefold ministry paradigm as you read this chapter.
3. Journal at least three benefits of team ministry as you consider this chapter.
4. Do a study on the New Testament church. Write a two page paper on what you learned and how the suggestions in this chapter are vital to a New Testament fivefold ministry church.

VISION CASTING

Vision Casting is the ability to clearly convey your divine vision from God to others where they can run with it by helping you to establish and advance it in the earth.

> *Habakkuk 2:1-3 I will stand upon my watch, and set me upon the tower, and will watch to see what he will say unto me, and what I shall answer when I am reproved. And the Lord answered me, and said, Write the vision, and make it plain upon tables, that he may run that readeth it. For the vision is yet for an appointed time, but at the end it shall speak, and not lie: though it tarry, wait for it; because it will surely come, it will not tarry.*

Vision Carrier is a person God has required to use to birth and/or advance a vision in the earth. Vision carriers embody the spiritual and natural ability to carry, birth, plant, plow, build, and establish God's plan and purpose in the earth; whether that be via ministry, business, organization, school, college, center, club, book, etc. This vision is instilled at birth. God gives clear instructions to the vision carrier for how to bring the vision to pass.

> *Romans 8:29-31 For whom he did foreknow, he also did predestinate to be conformed to the image of his Son, that he might be the firstborn among many brethren. Moreover whom he did predestinate, them he also called: and whom he called, them he also justified: and whom he justified, them he also glorified. What shall we then say to these things? If God be for us, who can be against us?*

Once God gives you the vision, you must be able to:

- Stand in what he has revealed to you.
- Watch over and be the gatekeeper of what he has revealed to you.
- Receive direction, correction, rebuke, wisdom, knowledge, counsel, strategy as needed from God and the overseers he has placed in your life concerning it (Reprove).
- Write the vision where others can read and understand it, see it and run with it.
- Articulate it so that others can receive an impartation from it.

- Cultivate the vision behind the scenes as God leads by planting it and working it, so that at the appointed time the truth of it will be revealed.
- Resist becoming weary as you plant and cultivate the vision in private with God, as though it appears to be tarrying, it is really being birthed out in prayer and in the spirit realm with God for its tangible day of revealing.

Vision casting is a vital part of the role of the main vision carrier. Sometimes the main vision carrier may be the apostle, and as others are under the vision of the apostle, their identity blueprints awaken and are released as they aide with the apostle's blueprint. Their identity blueprints are also released at an appointed time, thus becoming the expansion of what they are releasing as they journey and assist the apostle in the main vision.

I do want to state that the main vision carrier can also be any leader that God gives a fivefold ministry too. I would suggest though that as the main fivefold visionary, if you are not an apostle, to seek God for an apostle to walk with you as they will help guide you in birthing, establishing, and advancing your vision. They will be able to seek God concerning your identity, ministry blueprint, destiny and calling. They will be able to seek God for vision for you and aide you with releasing what God has granted to your hands. Moreover, as you connect with the apostle, seek God for other vision carriers that can help fill the other fivefold offices. It is essential to have these offices filled so that the vision can be properly governed through the kingdom of God for the building the body of Christ and cultivating revival reformation in the earth.

Vision casting is important for the vision carrier because they must be able to convey the vision to the other vision carriers. This is a part of your role as a pastor. God has a vision for your church. Your job is to help your parishioners get behind that vision.

The vision is instilled at birth.

The main vision carrier must have clarity from God regarding:

- Who you are – your identity? What is your destiny and calling? What is the character and standards God is requiring for you to walk in destiny with him? What he requires of you may not be the same as others. He may require more or less depending on your personality, generational propensities, and what he has called you to do in the earth. You have to be okay that what others may be able to do, go, etc., you may not be able to do or go. Even regarding some ministry scenes, events, and people. God may say no for you but it will appear okay for others. God knows what is needed to protect your identity, destiny and calling. Trust him and work on living the character and nature he has given for you as a lifestyle. (Study Samson – he could not cut his hair, but that was not the standard for everyone else. However, his strength and power resided in his hair, *(Judges 13-16)*.
- The vision God has given you – fivefold ministry blueprint. Is it a ministry, business, organization, human service or resource ministry, marketplace ministry, school, hub, cell group, training or equipping center, etc.? Sometimes there are multiple visions that God gives. Receive clarity for all of them and write a vision for each one of them. Search God for when to release each vision and who is a part of carrying each vision. Pace yourself and be okay with releasing each vision in his timing. This will help you not to get overwhelmed as the visions will flow together when they are released in God's timing. Be okay that you may plant a vision then release it to other vision carriers or successors to cultivate and advance in the earth. There are ministries I have planted only to give to others to awaken destiny in them.
- How does the fivefold ministry blueprint connect to your identity? What is the reason God desires this blueprint to be birthed through you? What is in you that God desires to uproot personally and generationally so that you can birth the vision through a pure well? What is the standard of the vision, as when you know this, you will know the reason for your personal standard? Remember you are the blueprint, so what is in you will be in the fivefold ministry vision. God is going to come for whatever is in you that will hinder the vision from being birthed in purity. This is the reason Jesus told Peter that the devil told him that the enemy desired to sift him as wheat. There were some things in Peter that he needed to be aware of that would impact the next SHIFT of his ministry. If you do not allow God to be honest with you in this area then you sow tares – ungodliness into the foundation of your ministry, and

it will eventually have to be gutted out or exposed. Better to gut it out now than later. And better to deal with it so that you will not be exposed as a contaminated ministry. SHIFT RIGHT NOW!

- Knowing how the fivefold blueprint is to be birthed in you also helps to identify your metron, your remnant, and sphere of influence. There are people, a region, and a sphere of influence that you are connected too. Sometimes, your very make up can help reveal this information. Sometimes, it can be revealed by your experiences. Sometimes, it can be revealed by what God is birthing through you.
- The current and long term direction and goals regarding your life and the vision – sometimes God may give this in measure. Be okay with that and seek him for clarity about what he does give. Do not add to the vision and be okay with telling people you will share more when you receive more. Be sensitive to the Holy Spirit with only sharing the vision as God leads and with who God leads you to share it with. He may have you withhold some portions of the vision for an appointed time as not to overwhelm the other vision carriers and some people may not be privy to the vision so be sensitive to this. The more you expose the vision to those that are not privy, the greater unnecessary warfare can be. It can also put you in a pit (Study the story of Joseph and his brothers (*Genesis 37-47*).
- Connecting with a covering, particularly an apostle who can adequately journey with you in releasing the vision. Let God do the connecting. Do not force it. He will send or reveal to you the apostle you need to connect to. I am an apostle. Yes, even as an apostle you will still need the connection of an overseer to journey with. When God revealed it was time to fully SHIFT into my ministry, he told me that as I go, he would send covering. I remained accountable to leaders and covenant partners until God connected me to the apostle that he wanted me to journey with. But I did not submit my ministry under anyone until this appointed time. At the appointed time, I was at home reading a book called "Spurned into Apostleship," when God told me to look on the back of the book, get the email of the author and contact her. I thought this was odd and I was very resistant. God rebuked me several times before I was obedient to what he was telling me to do. When I emailed her, I immediately received a response and she too was unctioned by the Lord to contact me concerning my email. Turns out, she had a ministry called "AIM – Apostles In

The Making." She trained, equipped, raised up and journeyed with apostles. Won't Jesus do it? He will do it for you. Your days of trying to get someone to connect with you are over. I decree your appointed covering is on the horizon. SHIFT RIGHT NOW!

- Who is to be the other vision carriers of the ministry? If these vision carriers are different from the fivefold officers, then who are the fivefold officers? Seek God for who they are. Do not choose them yourself. Seek him for who they are and wait on him to reveal them. I thought my vision carriers were seasoned saints who I had been doing ministry with for years. God revealed to me that my vision carriers were a group of millennials that knew nothing about fivefold ministry. I had to bring them into full salvation with God, train and equip them in their identity, destiny and calling, while also imparting the vision into them, and releasing the vision with them. I would not trade them for any other team in the world. They are the most fulfilling group of saints I have ever done ministry with.
- As God reveals the vision carriers, seek him for what their purpose and role is in your life personally and as vision carriers. As God reveals them, have them pray about their purpose as vision carriers in the ministry, their own identity blueprint and destiny and how it is connected to you and the ministry. Once they have had time to pray, meet with them and compare what God has spoken to the both of you. Set some tangible goals where they can begin to SHIFT and personally align as vision carriers.
- How to carry the vision with consistent joy, excitement and fulfillment so this can be instilled in others as the vision is conveyed, planted, cultivated, and released in the earth.
- How to convey the vision to the vision carriers, ministration team, partners, and sojourners that will come in seasons, so they will know their part in advancing the vision (You will learn about these teams in a later chapter).
- The blessings and benefits of fulfilling the personal and fivefold ministry mandate God has granted to all of you, and how it will impact each vision carrier, the ministry members, the community, region, body of Christ, and world at large.

As you receive clarity about this, then write the vision.

USE THE FOLLOWING FORMAT TO CREATE YOUR VISION PLAIN

From Dr. Taquetta Baker's book, "Sustaining The Vision."

I encourage you to type this plan as it is what banks, grant corporations, and investors will want to review as they consider connecting and investing in your vision.

- VISION TITLE
- VISION PURPOSE
- SCRIPTURE FOUNDATION & EXPLANATION FOR THE VISION
- MISSION STATEMENT
- FOUNDER'S INFORMATION
- CONTACT INFORMATION (Website, Email Address, Telephone Number, Street Address, Facebook, Twitter, Instagram, Blogging, LinkedIn info, etc.)
- ENTREPRENEUR SERVICES RENDERED (If there are multiple compartments of the vision, list them all in bullet point form and then answer the following questions under each compartment).
  - What will the ministry/business/organization be doing?
  - How will the ministry/business/organization go about fulfilling its vision?
  - What population will you be serving & what reasons have you chosen this population?
  - What makes your ministry/business/product unique from similar vision carriers?
  - What makes the ministry/business/organization unique from its competitors?
  - How often will this service occur?
  - What region or sphere of influence will this vision occur in?
  - What reasons this region or sphere of influence is essential to your vision?
- ENTREPRENEUR GUIDELINES:
  - GUIDELINES, CORE BELIEFS, AND REGULATIONS FOR THE MINISTRY/ORGANIZATION/BUSINESS (These are important in this day and time especially with

ministries being sued for their beliefs. These need to be written down and clearly given to each member, placed in your policy and procedure booklet, ministry booklet, and placed on your website so people will know exactly what they are committing to when they join your vision. Many people are sued because they have not conveyed this and then when people decide they want to sin or change God's word and try to get you to conform, they will say "well I did not know that was in your guidelines." You need to know and they need to know as this is your defense of free speech and right to your religious views).
- GUIDELINES FOR THOSE YOU WILL BE SERVING
- GUIDELINES FOR THOSE WHO WILL BE WORKING IN THE MINISTRY/ORGANIZATION/BUSINESS (What accountabilities and personal responsibilities do you need to put in place to keep the ministry in alignment with what God is requiring you to fulfill within the ministry?)

After writing the vision, it is time to start working with your team to vision cast and plant the vision.

> ***Ecclesiastes 3:1-3*** *To everything there is a season, and a time to every purpose under the heaven: A time to be born, and a time to die; a time to plant, and a time to pluck up that which is planted; A time to kill, and a time to heal; a time to break down, and a time to build up;*

> ***Jeremiah 1:10*** *See, I have this day set thee over the nations and over the kingdoms, to root out, and to pull down, and to destroy, and to throw down, to build, and to plant.*

Though not always the case, possible stages to initially releasing the vision.

1. Pray
2. Uproot, Tear Down, Destroy, Overthrow
3. Cultivate

4. Plant
5. Plow
6. Build
7. Plow Again
8. Advance

PRAY

All visions are birthed in prayer. This is the reason Habakkuk was on the wall watching to see what God was saying. He was acquiring the vision, and then continuously remaining in prayer as it was being cultivated. Prayer is your connection to God. It is also where you

- ❖ Identify those who you know may be a vision carrier and supporting team members and establish weekly or bi-monthly prayer calls or meetings where you begin to pray:

    - To plant seeds regarding the vision. Seeds are planted and hidden through a burying process, and cultivated for birthing, flourishing and harvesting. Do not uncover seeds before their time, as they will die or seed stealers will devour them (*Study Matthew 18*).
    - To birth the vision.
    - Into the identity, destiny, and calling of the main leader and vision carriers.
    - Gutting out personal and generational curses, strongholds, and cycles of vision carriers.
    - To birth and cultivate the character, nature, and fruit of God into the lives of all vision carriers, the vision itself, generational lines, and the region.
    - Over the metron, region and continuously establish God's government, eternal open heaven, and kingdom in that sphere.
    - Into the vision itself, and the visions, ministries, and business that God has granted into the hands of the vision carriers.
    - Over and release any prophetic words, promises, strategies God gives you regarding the vision.
    - Against any principalities, territorial spirits, powers, destiny killing spirits, witches, witchcraft, and demonic assignments that will strive to stifle the vision. Constantly seek God for

this information so you can be offensive against warfare that would try to come against the vision. The enemy will use people you know to combat the vision. Pray against how the enemy will use them to come against the vision.

The main vision carrier does not do all the praying but will give the vision carriers assignments on the prayer call, so they can take ownership of birthing, cultivating and growing the ministry. Prayer is ongoing. It never ceases. It is always in season. God will let you know when to war, intercede, decree, praise, give thanks, soak, rest in his presence as these and more are different ways to pray. But prayer is communion and is always in season. You will even learn as a fivefold minister that prayer is not just when you are in an isolated room with God. Prayer is all day. All throughout the day and night as you learn to walk in a lifestyle covenant with God. It would be good to acquire Dr. Taquetta Baker's book called, *"Prayers That Shift Atmospheres."* It is a weapons manual of how to pray and SHIFT in prayer with God, while SHIFTING everything you pray for and come in contact with. SHIFT!

Designate a strong prophetic prayer warrior to be over the prayer team. Give the vision carriers prayer assignments at least two days before the prayer call/meeting. Encourage them to get at least two scriptures they can pray into and seek God for what he is saying about the prayer points they are given so they can pray his heart and purpose. Encourage them to pray out loud, with boldness, and through the spirit over the assignment during their personal time, so they can pray through his confident spirit as they would pray as a team. They can be given feedback via text message as they pray or after they pray to further empower and train them in prayer. This is important in making sure each person is asserting authority in bravely towering in spiritual realms as they pray, and that you are doing a full work of breaking through as a team while praying together.

As the team spends a season birthing and planting the foundation of the fivefold blueprint, you can eventually begin to have prayer calls with members and the ministration team. You can even add them at times to the calls you already have with the vision carriers. As the ministry grows you can have prayer meetings several times a month with the vision carriers independently and with all members collectively. Prayer is the life source of your destiny and visions. Teach your ministry how to love prayer and how to pray successfully where things are transformed by

God and where we can see consistent tangible, kingdom manifestation. Instill this into the foundation of your vision so that it becomes your culture.

UPROOT, TEAR DOWN, DESTROY, OVERFLOW

In prayer meetings, services, and in one's daily walk this will manifest. Whatever is in the vision carriers, their generations, the land, atmosphere, regions, and spheres of influence, will be highlighted by the Holy Spirit and contended against. He will make sure the vision carriers have nothing in communion with what's in the land, atmosphere, region, etc. As he comes against it in you, he will also have you gut it out, tear it down, destroy, and overthrow it in your generations, and spheres of influence. You will be praying against, opposing it on your job, school, in the community, at family gatherings, etc. Your very lifestyle will be contending against darkness. So when you release the vision, it will be doing just that. Study Jeremiah and highlight how his very life contended against the wiles of the enemy.

CULTIVATE

As vision carriers come into their identity and understand their purpose regarding the vision, and as you all spend a season praying, begin to position the vision carriers within their perspective roles within the ministry and begin to cultivate and train them in these roles.

- ❖ Teach them responsibility and accountability to their roles and how their consistency or lack thereof, impacts their walk with the Lord, the team and the ministry.
- ❖ Train them in Godly character, how to live for God and how to have a daily lifestyle of destiny with God.
- ❖ As they show responsibility in these areas, begin to help them identify and cultivate them in their destiny and personal life's vision. Make sure they are operating consistently in the areas above before SHIFTING them into this season. They must have a healthy godly foundation where they are studying the word, praying, hearing independently from God, displaying his character and nature, and living his standard as a lifestyle. This is essential for the fivefold ministry vision, and for their own personal destinies and callings. Making sure they are consistent in these

areas will also aide you in further identifying them as a vision carrier. A vision carrier will want and pursue the heart and nature of God for the ministry. And even if they have times of struggle, their pursuit will be evident and heartfelt. If they have any other motives, it will manifest as they will have a difficult time SHIFTING into the character, nature and standards of the vision and no matter how hard they try, the fruit of the vision will not manifest.

- ❖ Train and equip your vision carriers as leaders, elders, in their perspective ministry positions, and eventually in their destiny and callings. Have people come in and train, attend online conferences, webinars, and classes, go to conferences and workshop together, and personally train them as God leads. It is very beneficial to create personal destiny tracks for each vision carrier where they have reading, writing, study, and prayer assignments that they are consistently working on to help cultivate their destiny and even bring forth their own life's vision. The track could include guidance and studies on areas they need to grow in (e.g. consistency, hearing from God, forgiving, trusting God, communication skills), working towards licensing and ordination, doing homework assignments related to their position within the ministry or launching their own vision. Give them specific dates to turn in assignments and meet with them monthly to assess where they are, to pray for them, and to further release and SHIFT them into their destiny. This is key, especially if you do not have consistent Sunday services, and for making sure your team is personally progressing in their personal destinies. They will always have something they will be working on and are not waiting on a service to cultivate them.
- ❖ Another wisdom key is when the vision carriers come to you with questions and issues, be mindful of what to immediately answer and what to send them back to search out with God. As the main vision carrier you are not God in their lives. The foundational pattern you set with them is what they will always expect. Being balanced is key. Also making sure their dependence is on God and not on you is key. It is important that all on the team know that you are journeying together in a lifestyle. so it is important to deal with matters as the spirit leads and not through emotion, false obligation, and false loyalty. Therefore, teach your team members to hear and lean on God by first asking them what is God saying before you offer wisdom or give them suggestions before you

share revelation and insight with them. Also, do not be quick to answer every text message and phone call. Sometimes God wants to speaks with the vision carrier. If you let him lead you on answering, they will sometimes hear from him before you even respond. I suggest the mentoring tracks and these wisdom keys regarding balanced interactions because they diminish burnout for the vision carrier. God is not calling you to be everything to everybody. Also how you and your team interact is cultivating a culture for how you all will interact with your members as the vision grows. You want to be able to role model healthy and balanced interaction so this will become the culture of your ministry.

PLANT

As the vision carriers are being trained, God will reveal a specific time to start planting the vision. He may have you start off having a service, overseeing a conference or event, doing trainings and workshops, completing assignments in the community, partnering with other ministries, businesses, and organizations to learn certain keys and information that will be vital to your ministry, launching a house or store front ministry, bible study etc. Whatever he has you and your team to do, SHIFT forth into it. He may have your vision carriers begin to plant their personal visions alongside of the main vision being planted. They are an expansion of you and the vision, so as long as God is in it, let them go for it. The main vision carriers may have to assist and support one another in their personal visions until God releases vision carriers under their personal ministries. Be okay with this and even create a calendar where you all can support and help one another plant as you SHIFT forth in your visions. You are doing life together so it is ok to grow and SHIFT together.

Sometimes when God gives you events to plant, he may say it is just for you and your team, or he may have you invite people. Sometimes people may not come and that is okay. You are still in the initial phases of your vision. God will be strategic about who to expose it to. Also God is developing your fervency and consistency. Ministry is about obedience, not about who shows up and partakes of it. There have been events that my team have done that we know SHIFTED the region and we were the only people there. There have been times that we know we are impacting people, lives, and families, though we were the only people there. There have events where we know we were planting for the future even though no one but us was there. We always plant and plow as if millions of people are present. We know we are birthing and bringing forth what is to come and we are building ourselves up to be sold out to God no matter what is occurring in our lives and ministries. The contingency is Jesus, not people, numbers, or circumstances. SHIFT RIGHT NOW! SHIFT!

As you plant, be cognizant of tares - ungodly characteristics, behaviors, curses, and patterns that cannot be instilled in the foundation of the vision. Deal with these areas quickly. Study the parable of the sower with your vision carriers (*Matthew 13:1-23, Mark :1-20, and Luke 8:4-15*). This will teach you all how to identify tares quickly and to uproot them.

In different seasons, God will give you and the vision carriers' specific characteristics to consistently plant and cultivate so they can be instilled in the foundation of the ministry. These characteristics are vital to the blueprint of the vision and it manifesting successfully. For example, in our ministry we have had seasons of planting and cultivating, purity, faith, compassion, humility, being sold out to the vision, miracles, signs, and wonders, revival reformation, relationship with Holy Spirit, being a Kingdom SHIFTER and etc. We would spend weeks even months on each characteristic, while studying, sowing, praying, fasting, and commanding them to become the foundation and identity of the vision. We would also be counter attacking and gutting out anything in us, the vision, and region that is contrary to the characteristic we are planting in that season.

PLOW
WHEWWWW! Plowing can be a challenging season but it is so important. The vision will go in and out of seasons of intense plowing. Plowing is an intense work of perseverance being done
in and through the vision carriers, for the bloodline, for the vision itself, for the land, region, and sphere of influence. It will also be for situations that will arise as you are planting, plowing, building, and advancing the vision and destinies and callings of those who are a part of the vision. Meditate on the definition and the scriptures on plowing. Ask God to give you visions and revelations regarding them. Journal your experiences and insights.

Dictionary.com defines *plowing* as:
1. to turn up the earth (an area of land) with a plow, especially before sowing
2. to cultivate, till, work, furrow, harrow, ridge, break up, turn up, hammer away
3. to move in a fast and uncontrolled manner
4. to plunge, bulldoze, hurtle, lurch, drive, run, barrel, impact
5. press, persevere, continue, insist, be diligent, be patient, go the distance, carrying
6. wade, flounder, toil, plod, plug away, stay the course, stick at it, soldier on, hang on, bash on
7. continue steadily despite difficulties or warnings to stop

> *Luke 9:62* But Jesus said to him, No one, after putting his hand to the plow and looking back, is fit for the kingdom of God.

> *Ezekiel 36:6* For, behold, I am for you, and I will turn unto you, and ye shall be tilled and sown.

> *The Message Bible* Do you see? I'm back again. I'm on your side. You'll be plowed and planted as before!

> *Isaiah 28:24-26* Does he who plows for sowing plow continually? Does he continue to plow and harrow the ground after it is smooth? When he has leveled its surface, does he not cast abroad [the seed of] dill or fennel and scatter cummin [a seasoning], and put the wheat in rows, and barley in its intended place, and spelt [an inferior kind of wheat] as the border? [And he trains each of them correctly] for his God instructs him correctly and teaches him.

> *Amos 9:13* Behold, days are coming," declares the LORD, "When the plowman will overtake the reaper And the treader of grapes him who sows seed; When the mountains will drip sweet wine And all the hills will be dissolved.

> *Job 4:8* According to what I have seen, those who plow iniquity And those who sow trouble harvest it.

> *1Corinthians 9:10* Or saith he it altogether for our sakes? For our sakes, no doubt, this is written: that he that ploweth should plow in hope; and that he that thresheth in hope should be partaker of his hope.

BUILD

Be careful how you build, when you build, and where you build. As wisdom is key to building.

> ***1Corinthians 3:10** By the grace God has given me, I laid a foundation as a wise master builder, and someone else is building on it. But each one must be careful how he builds.*

Dictionary.com *defines* build:
1. to make or construct (especially something complex) by assembling and joining parts or materials
2. to establish, increase, or strengthen (often followed by up)
3. to mold, form, or create
4. to engage in the art, practice, or business of building
5. to increase or develop toward a maximum, as of intensity, tempo, or magnitude
6. build in / into, to build or incorporate as part of something else
7. build up
   A. to develop or increase
   B. to strengthen
   C. to prepare in stages
   D. to fill in with houses
   E. to praise or flatter

> ***Proverbs 24:3** By wisdom a house is built, And by understanding it is established.*

<u>Built in this passage is *bana* and means:</u>
1. to build (literally and figuratively): — (begin to) build(-er), obtain children, to have children,
2. make, repair, rebuilt, establish, set, restore exiles, make permanent, to cause an continuous

It is interesting that this passage references obtaining or making children. When you build something, you are building a legacy! COME ON! WHEWWWW! SHIFT RIGHT NOW! SHIFT!

- ✓ You need wisdom and understanding to build a successful legacy.
- ✓ You need vision and strategy.
- ✓ You need the blueprint and the revelation to bring the blueprint to pass.

As you SHIFT into the building stage, you need vision carriers around you that have the heart of God for you and for the vision, where you are not constantly having to prove to them what God has said, that they are called to be a part, and need to be consistent in what God has said. Vision carriers seek God concerning you and their purpose in the ministry so they have clear revelation of their purpose, and are able to build you up as you build. They are built up by you and the vision as they help you to build. Any other posture will drain and distract you and the vision, as your focus will be constantly trying to get them to align rather than allowing the purpose of the Lord to be the alignment that guides the building process. Therefore, make sure your vision carriers are ready and equipped to build.

What you are building has to be able to spiritually and naturally withstand:
- Weather conditions
- Ground conditions
- Trials, tribulations, wars, & warfare
- Specific uses
- Inspections
- Wear and tear (aesthetics)
- Its purpose and need

What you build has to be able to:
- Gift and bestow gifts - Apostolic Ministry
- Speak the vision – Prophetic Ministry
- Save, deliver, & heal – Evangelist Ministry
- Instruct, train & equip – Teacher Ministry
- Shepherd the Sheep – Pastoral Ministry
- Protect and be a protector - Guard
- Cover and be a covering - Govern
- Shelter and be a shelter - Refuge
- Equip and be an equipper - Build up
- Launch and be a launcher - Send forth

When you are building for God, he is the only one who gets to dictate how you build and what you focus on while you build (***Study Nehemiah 6:9-14***). Some plans he gives you ahead of time and others you learn as you BUILD with him. Nehemiah was sought after four times to come down and focus on something that was not a part of the current building vision. A fifth pursuit of Nehemiah came with accusation and misperceptions that sounded as if they could have merit. Nehemiah knew they were not of the Lord and were sent to instill fear and weakness so they would not build through the strength of the Lord. The visionary always carries the character and nature of the BUILDING vision. This is how Nehemiah knew this was a trick of the enemy. He had become the identity of the plan before he even began BUILDING IT!

The enemy would want you to come down and defend yourself against false prophecy, delusions, and conspiracies, but do not do it. You have all the defense and prophecies you need at this current time and in the current dimension to which you are BUILDING. Anything contrary to what God is speaking is a false vision of infiltration setting you up to be deterred, stifled, delayed, or destroyed. Do not get into prideful petty tiffs that are not your battle. Stay focused and BUILD IT!

As you build, do not focus on who is a hater. When you focus on them hating on you, you regress to demonstrating ungodly character of offense and revenge that justifies their actions. When you stay focused on being God's example and martyr for his glory, you exemplify Godly character and a lifestyle that draws them to Jesus. Haters are meant to watch and hate as they need deliverance. Your lifestyle is the key to their breakthrough. Stop preaching against and being aggravated about what they are saying and doing and be you. You - your God identity - your lifestyle example - is the blueprint to them being drawn to the foot of Jesus.

- BUILDERS are focused on the right things
- BUILDERS represent God
- BUILDERS are on display for God's glory
- BUILDERS do not come off the wall for petty warfare
- BUILDERS love the heck out of people
- BUILDERS love the devil out of people
- BUILDERS know that haters are part of the process
- BUILDERS are not proving anything just doing God's thing
- BUILDERS stand and are God's example
- BUILD yourself in God confidence so you can focus
- BUILD and chill in it
- BUILDERS rest in letting the BUILDING speak and preach for itself
- BUILDING saves souls as even your haters need saving
- BUILD IT!

As you build, do not shortchange or cut corners by using that which is cheap and convenient. Cheap labor can be pricey in the long run. Convenient labor can cause you to have to gut out and rebuild foundations and portions of your vision that could have been done correctly in the first place had you not cheated the vision. Not cheating the vision is about integrity and godly standards, and building through the nature, character, and identity of God. Compromising your building foundation in these areas, results in building through that which is flawed, erred, crooked, off centered, indifferent, conflicting, opposing to your vision; which eventually shows itself through cracks, weeds, and tares, intertwining in that which you are building.

- ❖ Say no to short cuts
- ❖ Say no to cheap labor
- ❖ Say no to people who lack integrity
- ❖ Say no to people who lack the vision standard
- ❖ Say no to wavering in what God is saying
- ❖ Say no to compromising what God is saying
- ❖ Say no to quick building that sidetracks the vision

Stay the course and build God's way. SHIFT!

As you BUILD the vision:
- Build on Jesus the chief cornerstone
- Build through a healthy identity & blueprint
- Build a healthy foundation
- Build healthy framing and insulation
- Build fortified solid walls
- Build through heaven's government & covering
- Build sufficient doorways & entryways
- Build people
- Build team & teamwork
- Build covenant relationship & fellowship
- Build Godly character & integrity
- Build through the fruit of the spirit
- Build leaders & vision carriers
- Build destinies & to reform regions
- Build faith
- Build in love & love for the vision
- Build stamina to persevere

- Build unwavering relentless praise & worship
- Build in spirit & truth
- Build with the mind of Christ
- Build from heaven to earth - build his kingdom
- Build inside the glory
- Build despite challenges
- Build to demolish darkness
- Build set a part
- Build for his glory
- SHIFT RIGHT NOW AND BUILD! SHIFT!

PLOW AGAIN! Remember plowing will come all throughout the vision. SHIFT!

ADVANCE

Advancing denotes a time of progressing and expanding what you have planted, plowed and built. You will SHIFT in and out of seasons of advancement.

Dictionary.com defines advance as:
1. to move or bring forward
2. to bring into consideration or notice; suggest; propose
3. to improve; further
4. to raise in rank; promote
5. to raise in rate or amount; increase
6. to bring forward in time; accelerate

These will be seasons of favor, blessings, increase, multiplication, reaping and harvest. It also will be seasons of further driving and pruning, defining, solidifying and accelerating what you have built. It is important to take notice of what is occurring during seasons of advancement. You want to guard your harvest as the enemy will send people and situations to try to stifle, steal and kill your harvest. People and demonic assignments will come to drain your time of advancement by having you taking on causes that are not of God, having you sow into unfruitful grounds, having you focused on present, immature, and fleeting expenditures rather than future investment. People, especially loved ones, will be used in effort to guilt you into petty, ungodly, and rescuing investments. Be mindful of how the enemy will come, as the greater reason is to replant generational curses, cycles, and patterns that you all as vision carriers have already plucked up and overthrown. The enemy will strive to erect walls, roadblocks and barriers to hinder advancement. Be mindful to seek God for demonic assignments as you really want to be offensive in guarding your seasons of advancement.

PRUNING
When building a fivefold vision, pruning will occur. Pruning is part of the fivefold process and will occur all throughout the advancement of the vision.

> *John 15:2 Every branch in Me that does not bear fruit, He takes away; and every branch that bears fruit, He prunes it so that it may bear more fruit.*

Prune means *"to cleanse, to purify of filth, to expiate (atone, amend, make good), to free what is not healthy, beneficial, or necessary."* Pruning is caused by an actual cutting and removing, ridding, or clearing of a person, thing, or matter. Pruning is for our good but does not feel good. The pruning can feel like pain, grief, loss, or death as an actual severing is taking place. After a time these feelings are replaced with healing, refreshing, restoration, and clarity regarding the pruning.

Reasons pruning may occur:
- Pruning the lives of the main vision carriers, and the members. Pruning family members, friends, behaviors, pet peeves, ideologies and beliefs, character flaws, activities, desires, needs, curses, culture trends, worldliness, sin issues, demonic strongholds, religion, tradition. Some of this pruning will have nothing to do with ungodliness but may occur simply because it is not needful for the SHIFT God is doing, where God is taking you, and how God will use you. Also when SHIFTING with God, he will provide and restore everything needed for your destiny journey. SHIFT!

> *Matthew 10:5-10 These twelve Jesus sent forth, and commanded them, saying, Go not into the way of the Gentiles, and into any city of the Samaritans enter ye not: But go rather to the lost sheep of the house of Israel. And as ye go, preach, saying, The kingdom of heaven is at hand. Heal the sick, cleanse the lepers, raise the dead, cast out devils: freely ye have received, freely give. Provide neither gold, nor silver, nor brass in your purses, Nor scrip for*

your journey, neither two coats, neither shoes, nor yet staves: for the workman is worthy of his meat.

- When SHIFTING from a pastoral to a fivefold ministry paradigm. Those that do not want change, understand change, or are resistant to change may leave. The ministry will become smaller due to pruning then will grow as it begins to awaken through the new vision. The present vision may also be pruned as things that are not fivefold or are not beneficial to the new vision will be pruned. Please know that God will add, restore, and do exceedingly in his timing. The pruning will be for your good.

    - ≈ ***Proverbs 10:22*** *The blessing of the Lord, it maketh rich, and he addeth no sorrow with it.*
    - ≈ ***Romans 8:28*** *And we know that all things work together for good to them that love God, to them who are the called according to his purpose.*
    - ≈ ***Ephesians 3:20*** *Now unto him that is able to do exceeding abundantly above all that we ask or think, according to the power that worketh in us.*

- When vision carriers are not submissive to carrying the vision as God requires or if they do not want the vision carrying position. This type of pruning occurs so that God can build a healthy foundation that can sustain the vision. When vision carriers are opposing to the vision, God will remove them to preserve the healthiness of the foundation. This is because what is in vision carriers is rooted in the foundation of the vision.

    Matthew 27:3-5 3 *Then Judas, which had betrayed him, when he saw that he was condemned, repented himself, and brought again the thirty pieces of silver to the chief priests and elders, saying, I have sinned in that I have betrayed the innocent blood. And they said, What is that to us? see thou to that. And he cast down the pieces of silver in the temple, and departed, and went and hanged himself).*

- When the ministry SHIFTS times and seasons and God shakes out anything or anyone that cannot SHIFT to the next season of ministry.

> *Leviticus 25:3-4 Six years you shall sow your field, and six years you shall prune your vineyard and gather in its crop, but during the seventh year the land shall have a sabbath rest, a sabbath to the LORD; you shall not sow your field nor prune your vineyard.*

- When people become disgruntled, disobedient, sinful, dishonorable, defiant, anti-Christ, reprobate. The original Israelites that let Egypt in Moses era were not allowed to enter the promise land because they engaged in some of these behaviors. They were pruned from the very promises they spent 40 years pursuing. Only their seed entered the promise land. (Study ***Deuteronomy 1:19-45***) Please know God will protect the vision. He will use you to establish it but not allow you to reap the fruit of it. Should he decide to do this, let it be because you have finished your course rather sin or character issues.

- God will require pruning in season. He will require a pruning people, positions, parts of the vision even those that appear to be flourishing or deemed beneficial.

    > ***Hebrew 12:27*** *And this word, Yet once more, signifieth the removing of those things that are shaken, as of things that are made, that those things which cannot be shaken may remain.*

- God will use pruning as a weapon of judgment.

    - ≈ ***Isaiah 2:4*** *And He will judge between the nations, And will render decisions for many peoples; And they will hammer their swords into plowshares and their spears into pruning hooks Nation will not lift up sword against nation, And never again will they learn war.*
    - ≈ ***Joel 3:10*** *Beat your plowshares into swords And your pruning hooks into spears; Let the weak say, "I am a mighty man."*

- God will prune to rid experiences from the remembrance of the vision.

    > ***Isaiah 65:17*** *For behold, I will create new heavens and a new earth. The former things will not be remembered, nor will they come to mind.*

- God will prune to protect the generational work and name of the main vision carrier/s. He will not allow their work to be tainted or destroyed by ungodly people and experiences.

> **Isaiah 66:22** *"For just as the new heavens and the new earth, which I will make, will endure before Me," declares the LORD, "so your descendants and your name will endure.*

Homework Explorations:

1. I know this chapter entailed a lot of information. This information is to be implemented overtime so you will do life with this chapter. It is really vital to spend consistent time seeking God for vision and continuously using this chapter to plant, cultivate, plow, build and advance your destiny, calling, and life's vision. Decreeing revelation and insight from God regarding your vision is invading you even now in Jesus name. SHIFT!
2. Journal what you learned about writing a vision plan.
3. If you are in a season of being able to write a vision plan, do just that using the information in this chapter.
4. Study and journal on all the scriptures suggested throughout this chapter.
5. Journal what you learned about planting, uprooting, cultivating, plowing, building and advancing your vision.
6. Journal what stage of the vision you are in and seek God for insight on how to successfully navigate this stage. Journal what he says.
7. Journal your thoughts and experiences on pruning. Really spend time seeking God to embrace pruning as part of your lifestyle as a fivefold visionary.

CREATING MEASURABLE BLUEPRINT GOALS

As you are releasing your fivefold vision in your ministry, region, and sphere of influence, set goals that can be measured. You want to be able to measure:

- The people - remnant - you are impacting
- The land, communities, and region you are impacting
- The spheres of influence you are impacting (e.g. education, entertainment and media, political, spiritual, business and economics, social, family and generational legacy)
- Your success, failures and progress
- The necessary changes that may be needed to strengthen your impact

> ***Revelations 11:15*** *And the seventh angel sounded; and there were great voices in heaven, saying, The kingdoms of this world are become the kingdoms of our Lord, and of his Christ; and he shall reign for ever and ever.*
>
> ***The Amplified Bible*** *The seventh angel then blew [his] trumpet, and there were mighty voices in heaven, shouting, The dominion (kingdom, sovereignty, rule) of the world has now come into the possession and become the kingdom of our Lord and of His Christ (the Messiah), and He shall reign forever and ever (for the eternities of the eternities)!*

The goals you set will help to establish whether the kingdoms of this world are becoming the kingdoms of God. It will help to determine whether you are:

- Sufficiently impacting the people and sphere you are ministering in.
- Pursuing, overtaking, and even recovering the land, people and sphere that the enemy has ensnared through worldly affairs.
- Establishing God's kingdom in the midst of the world's kingdom such that you draw people out of darkness to God. We hear a lot about overtaking mountains of the world but really God does not want the devil's mess. He wants us to establish the purity of his kingdom where it is clear that he is reigning and governing in the earth. We must also be realistic that as we infiltrate the world systems, unless we establish our own mountains, there is only a measure of overtaking we can do. This is because we are required to respect and operate within the laws of the world's systems. But

many of these laws are contrary to God's law so we end up overtaking in measure or compromising in order to make an impact. But when we establish our own mountains, they can be governed by the laws and standards of God. And we can impact through the fullness of the vision and goals he gives us.
- ❖ Releasing your vision efficiently or if changes need to be made to improve productivity.
- ❖ In the timing, momentum or even the correct sphere or region of the Lord such that you experience progress and success as you release your visions.

As we consider measurable blueprint goals you would first need to have:

- A blueprint vision - The foundational blueprint God has given you for your ministry, business, organization.
- A mission's or movement statement or focus - A statement that includes one to three sentences describing the purpose of your vision.
- A foundational scripture for your blueprint - Scriptural foundation that grounds and confirms your vision.
- Measurable blueprint goals - Three to six measurable goals would be sufficient to provide a terminal point towards the results you want to achieve. (See Taquetta Baker's "Sustaining The Vision Workbook" for more information on writing visions and goals).

These goals should be visited at least every three to six months where you are examining their success.

Be mindful that with some visions it takes a while to plant, plow and build. So the fruit of a vision may not be immediately evident. It is therefore important to only change or add a goal if God is leading you.

It is also important to only add or change a goal where it is in alignment with the vision. Do not add anything God is not saying. As what works for others, may not work or be for you.

Make sure you are not operating in a microwave mentality. It has taken me years to plant and plow Kingdom Shifters Ministries. Originally, I did not have all of the blueprint. And some of what I knew was much bigger than I had the time or manpower for. But God would release parts of the vision in season, while implementing measurable obtainable goals that did not overwhelm the areas of the vision I had already released. Moreover, what appeared to take others days and months to do, sometimes took me years. It was because the standards that God gave me regarding my blueprint and what I had to uproot out of myself, my generations, my regions and spheres of influence was much different than others. Therefore, my goals and progression was different than others.

Sometimes people are building without planting and establishing a solid foundation.

> ***Jeremiah 1:10*** *See, I have this day set thee over the nations and over the kingdoms, to root out, and to pull down, and to destroy, and to throw down, to build, and to plant.*

Many are bypassing the work of plowing which entails rooting out, pulling down, destroying, and throwing down so that the vision can be established in good soil and on a solid foundation. You do not want to have to go back and redo the foundation or plow in areas that were rushed, overlooked, or missed because you rushed the vision. Be at peace with the momentum God provides for achieving the goals and visions he has given you. Your blueprint operates best and in full authority when all of it represents God. Want to please God and manifest his blueprint more than you want to prove or reveal your blueprint in the earth. SHIFT!

Homework Explorations:
1. Spend time with God concerning this chapter.
2. Journal what he shares.
3. Write a vision plan, mission statement, foundation scripture and measurable obtainable goals regarding the blueprint he gives you.
4. Seek him for timing and be obedient in implementing what he is saying regarding releasing the vision and working on your measurable goals.
5. Share what God has given you with your overseer and accountability partners so they can encourage, support and keep you accountable to what God has granted to your hands.
6. SHIFT AGAIN! SHIFT!

BUILDING A FIVEFOLD MINISTRY TEAM

The greatest power of a fivefold ministry is TEAM!

Apostles or main leaders must administrate and release the blueprint to the foundational vision carrying team. The foundational vision carrying team must administrate and release the blueprint to the supporting team and members. This is essential in making sure the vision is a fivefold paradigm where the body of members are doing their part to assist in successfully supporting and advancing the vision in the earth (*Study 1Corinthians 12:12-31*).

> **1Corinthians 12:12** *For as the body is one, and hath many members, and all the members of that one body, being many, are one body: so also is Christ.*

Initially, the apostle and the foundational vision carriers may have to complete double duties. This will be more to set order, establish a pure fivefold foundation, and role model the blueprint. If the ministry is small, then the foundational vision carriers will have to perform multiple duties until the ministry grows and they effectively train the members to be responsible, accountable, and equipped in walking with the Lord, ministry, and destiny. Generally, this is where those following the apostle/leader are exposed, identified and set apart as true vision carriers. A vision carrier will have the following attributes:

- ❖ A relentless heart for God.
- ❖ An uncompromising heart for the apostle or main leader of the vision.
- ❖ An uncompromising heart for the vision and wanting to see it come to pass.
- ❖ A vigorous work ethic to labor for the vision, even with working multiple positions, completing whatever duties necessary, laboring steadfastly behind the scenes to make sure the vision is a success.
- ❖ Self-sacrificing for the sake of the leader, the team and the vision.
- ❖ Sold out to God and his kingdom with an understanding that this is destiny living.
- ❖ Has an understanding that the vision is a part of his/her destiny and possibly their heritage.

- Covenant minded - recognizing that his or her actions reflect and impact God, the kingdom, the team, and the vision.
- Reliable and trustworthy.
- Spiritually balanced, mentally stable; can weather or learn to weather challenging seasons and life situations.
- Disciplined or open to SHIFT into a disciplined God lifestyle.
- Secret keeper. Able to keep the secrets and guard gates of the vision, the other vision carriers, and the believers that they oversee.
- Teachable and ever learning.
- Want what God desires for their lives, the vision, and the lives they labor with and minister too.
- Ever ready, determined, relentless, in SHIFTING into their God ordained identity, and pursuing their destiny and calling, while desiring the same for others.
- Truth bearers and are able to receive truth.
- Able to accept constructive criticism, and implement it quickly to remain in alignment with the momentum to God personally and as it relates to the vision.
- Pliable, flexible, supple, adaptable, adjusting readily to change to SHIFT with God and the vision.
- Chosen by God, not man and not because they are gifted. They possess an innate call of duty to the vision at hand. Even if they do not want the call, it will be evident that God chose them. They will fit inside the blueprint of the vision even if they struggle with their identity and calling. Who they are will be a blessing, expansion, and advancement of the vision. It will not sway, deplete, or alter the vision.
- Love purity, righteousness, holiness, healthiness, divine order and sound doctrine.
- Able to honor and esteem others higher than themselves, and biblically honor and trust those who are their leaders.
- Innate capacity to embody the vision and actually become a living representation of it. This is vital as God will gut out of the vision carriers everything that cannot be in the foundation of the ministry vision. He will come for character issues, sins and ungodly behaviors, and generational curses and patterns within the vision carrier. As they are rooted out of the vision carriers and the vision carriers plant the vision, they are thus gutted out of the ministry

vision. With this design, God will be seeking to establish a pure foundation for the ministry vision to be built on where the gates of hell cannot prevail against it.

Matthew 16:18 And I say also unto thee, That thou art Peter, and upon this rock I will build my church; and the gates of hell shall not prevail against it. And where hell cannot find any place to dwell in the ministry vision.

John 14:30 Hereafter I will not talk much with you: for the prince of this world cometh, and hath nothing in me.

Jesus knew he was the ultimate vision carrier for salvation - saving the world. He knew he could not have anything in him that was of the devil and this was essential to overthrowing his kingdom and establishing the foundation of salvation in the earth.

Luke 5:19 And when they could not find by what way they might bring him in because of the multitude, they went upon the housetop, and let him down through the tiling with his couch into the midst before Jesus.

All these attributes will have to be taught, but as the members "catch" the vision, the true vision carriers will run with it. For a time, they may battle their unyielding flesh, their stubborn will, their inner man not feeling worthy of the call, generational curses and patterns, and familiar spirits speaking against their true identity and destiny. As these godly attributes are embedded in their foundation, and the foundation of the vision, the true vision carriers will arise and it will be evident that they are vision carriers. Even if they make mistakes and are challenged by their call, they will acknowledge their need for change, accept constructive criticism and guidance for change, and keep plowing until they become the ministry vision. They will have a heart and yearning to be, have, and do, all of what God requires of them. You will SHIFT from convincing and validating them to them demonstrating and becoming the tangible truth of a vision carrier.

As the vision grows, there are some duties that apostles or the main leader, and even the foundational vision carriers may not have time to do. These duties should be delegated to wise, loyal, able bodied, integral members. The apostle/leader and even the vision carriers can then be free to be with the Lord, so they can receive more revelation and guidance on building, equipping and advancing the members and the vision.

> *Acts 6:1-3 And in those days, when the number of the disciples was multiplied, there arose a murmuring of the Grecians against Hebrews, because their widows were neglected in the daily ministration. Then the twelve called the multitude of the disciples unto them, and said, It is not reason that we should leave the word of God, and serve tables. Wherefore, brethren, look ye out among you seven men of honest report, full of the Holy Ghost and wisdom, whom we may appoint over this business. But we will give ourselves continually to prayer, and to the ministry of the word.*

The greatest power of a fivefold ministry is team!

Let me take a moment to speak directly to the apostle or main leader of the ministry vision.

- ❖ The team will have to be okay that you may plan an event or require the completion of a task, but they will have to oversee it.
- ❖ Your team is called, equipped, and capable, as you should be consistently training them. So be okay with allowing them to oversee as God leads.
- ❖ Be okay that there will be some events and tasks assignments you will not attend. As the main vision carrier, every part of the vision is weighing on you in the spirit realm. You accompany this with gatekeeping and other factors, and already you are doing the most. No one knows the spiritual weight of that but another apostle or main leader. Apostles administer and carry the vision, but they are not always in the midst of it. Be mindful to have your team shutdown chatter of people speaking against you regarding this. As when they do, they are revealing that they do not understand the apostle's mandate. Yet, their words will come to afflict and whip you for not being something they think you should be. You will feel those lashings in your body if they are not dealt with.

LEADERSHIP SOUL & VISION GOVERNING

When you are the main vision carrier, your relationship to the other vision carriers and members of the vision will be different. You will not be making decisions about them or the vision through your heart and love for them and ministry, but through your spirit and as a governor of their soul and the vision. This is a different posture than a regular believer because relationship, kinship, history, loyalty, fondness, your heart and love for the person, and even covenant with them, cannot override God's government of their soul, the vision, and will and purpose for their lives and the vision.

> *Hebrews 13:17* *Obey them that have the rule over you, and submit yourselves: for they watch for your souls, as they that must give account, that they may do it with joy, and not with grief: for that is unprofitable for you.*

<u>Rule</u> is *hēgeomai* in Greek and means:
1. to lead, i.e. command (with official authority); figuratively, to deem, i.e. conside
2. account, (be) chief, count, esteem, governor
3. judge, have the rule over, suppose, think
4. to have authority over, leading as respects influence, controlling in counsel, overseers or leaders of the churches
5. the leader in speech, chief, spokesman

This position is not to be taken lightly and is to be handled with conscious care. It requires balance, extreme sensitivity to the spirit, being able to see the people as God sees them, while possessing the divine ability to govern and engage them through his vision despite relationship and fellowship.

Jesus kept clear boundaries in how he governed the souls of the disciples and the vision of him dying on the cross. No matter how familiar they would become with him, he would guide them back to them being saved, being ready to walk in their purpose and destiny, the understanding that he would not be with them always, and them having to carry the fruit and gospel of his vision after he died and was resurrected to the right hand of the father.

- ✓ There were times he would rebuke them to restore them to this purpose.

- ✓ There were times he would share parables.
- ✓ There were times he would teach and instruct.
- ✓ There were times he would role model this via ministry.
- ✓ There were times he would role model this in servitude unto them and through balanced fellowship.
- ✓ There were times he would activate and release them in doing as they saw him do.

Though Jesus was friendly, fellowshipped and broke bread with them, expressed his love for them, let them lay on his bosom, had covenant with them, empowered and partook of their identity, destinies, and callings, was a ministry partner to them, he never SHIFTED out of his governing seat as savior. All of what he gave the disciples was through his ruling seat of the vision of salvation and savior coming to pass.

Jesus was such a governor of souls, his purpose, and godly vision, that he did not allow family members to SHIFT him from his seat of rulership.

> *Matthew 12:46-50 While he yet talked to the people, behold, his mother and his brethren stood without, desiring to speak with him. Then one said unto him, Behold, thy mother and thy brethren stand without, desiring to speak with thee. But he answered and said unto him that told him, Who is my mother? and who are my brethren? And he stretched forth his hand toward his disciples, and said, Behold my mother and my brethren! For whosoever shall do the will of my Father which is in heaven, the same is my brother, and sister, and mother.*

This appeared as if Jesus was denying and dishonoring his family, but none of that was occurring. In that moment he was not son or brother, he was governor of souls and the vision. In this posture, kinship does not override the authority and kingdom of God. They wanted him to SHIFT out of this posture and he was demonstrating that you never SHIFT from being the gatekeeper of souls and God's vision, not even for family.

This is key for the main vision carrier because you will realize that though you have relationship with those you lead, you cannot allow familiarity to SHIFT you into making decisions regarding souls and the vision out of,

- ✓ Natural duty or natural laws.
- ✓ Family or cultural traditions and trends.
- ✓ Relationship to people.

- ✓ Their longevity in your life and to the ministry.
- ✓ Positions of people in the ministry.
- ✓ The response or lack of response from people.
- ✓ How they respond to your seat and mandate.

Your alliance and allegiance is to God first and to those who are aligning with the purpose and will of God. Even then you are leading and guiding them to God regarding that. They should display honor regarding the position you have in their life first, and allow anything else they are allowed to be and get from you to be filtered through that governmental position.

Jesus called the disciples friend, he never SHIFTED from his office seat as governor of their souls and the vision.

> *John 15:12-15 This is my commandment, That ye love one another, as I have loved you. Greater love hath no man than this, that a man lay down his life for his friends. Ye are my friends, if ye do whatsoever I command you. Henceforth I call you not servants; for the servant knoweth not what his lord doeth: but I have called you friends; for all things that I have heard of my Father I have made known unto you.*

Jesus was telling the disciples that the greatest love he could bestow upon them was to fulfill the vision of laying down his life for them. This was his mandate in the earth. *Leaders whatever your mandate is, that is the greatest gift of love you could give those you lead and the world at large.* Jesus said this is how he displays his friendship. It was not in doing what others wanted him to do, being what others wanted him to be, catering to what others thought he should be, succumbing to ungodly ideologies and characteristics so that others could deem him loving and friendly, continuously proving to others that he loved and deemed them as friends. It was fulfilling his purpose in the earth. *Leaders you fulfill your role of friendship and love by being who God told you to be to people.* Because the disciples were able to receive Jesus in the truth of his identity, destiny and calling, their role SHIFTED from servants to friends. He thus opened his heart to sharing his godly secrets with them because they honored who he was and had SHIFTED to being his friends. *Leaders, your friends are those who can honor what God has spoken and is doing through your life.* And even then, you are not sharing personal information about yourself, you are sharing secrets of the Father that they can glean and mature from. SHIFT RIGHT NOW!

I shared this revelation to say that it will be important to ask God to identify true godly friends and to bring you godly friends. As you will not be able to get personal needs and desires met from most of those you are overseeing. Your role as leader is to give them God and give them vision. Even in fellowship, there will be boundaries that you will not be able to cross. For familiarity breeds challenges of dishonor and disregard. You will have to identify who are spiritual friends like Jesus spoke about above and who are personal confidants. Your personal confidants will have to be able to respect your role as the main vision carrier first and not expect personal favors, nor should they overstep protocols and order just because of their position in your life. They should be clearly identified by God and be able to distinguish when they are engaging with their leader and with their personal friend. If the person has challenges with this then they are not called to be a personal confidant in your life. The two of you are probably forcing a role of relationship that is not of God but you are trying to make it be God. This could result in offense, usurping, and/or this person using the personal information they have had privy too against you. It is important to be clear about who labors among you and what their role is to your life and to the vision. SHIFT!

Leaders you fulfill your role of friendship and love by being who God told you to be to people.

1Thessalonians 5:12-13 *And we beseech you, brethren, to know them which labour among you, and are over you in the Lord, and admonish you; And to esteem them very highly in love for their work's sake. And be at peace among yourselves.*

If you already had relationship with those you are now leading, they will have to learn how to honor, and receive from you through this new position of governing and authority.
- ✓ They will begin to see that they are not just talking to their friend, sister, brother, but a governor of their souls and the vision. They will also discern that your role, interaction, and the relationship dynamics will change to accommodate the leadership office you have SHIFTED into.

- ✓ They will soon realize that what they knew about you and how you engaged with them is now different because of your elevated seat as vision carrier. You will change as you evolve as the main vision carrier. Your character, personality, destiny, calling, will shape and evolve to embody your office.

- ✓ They recognize that you are now guiding them in their destiny lifestyle and through the vision, and that you are a governor and covering for their lives.
- ✓ They realize that you are a representative of God and his authority to them in the earth. Though you may at times be on the side of them as a brother or sister in Christ, family member, etc., you are FIRST and FOREMOST overseer of their lives and souls.

As the main vision carrier, you will recognize that they are your covenant relationship partners but may not necessarily be your confidants. They are confidants of one another in their covenants but they may not necessary be that for you if they cannot handle your new role. You can fellowship with them at times as God leads, but in others times, you may have to say "no" to keep balance with breeding familiarity or because God wants to spend that time with you. This SHIFT is a process that everyone will have to become used to. It will be important to communicate and teach so that people will know what is occurring, how to navigate the change and their emotions, and how to SHIFT to the role and posture God is requiring. Please note that the relationship will still be fulfilling though it may be different. God is always about blessing and producing success in our lives.

> ***Romans 1:11-12 The Amplified Bible*** *For I long to see you so that I may share with you some spiritual gift, to strengthen and establish you; that is, that we may be mutually encouraged and comforted by each other's faith, both yours and mine.*

<u>*Homework Explorations:*</u>
1. Journal your thoughts and experience regarding this chapter.
2. What are four ways you can resist becoming familiar with your leader? What reasons is this important?
3. Journal the qualities you desire in a personal confidant. Spend time asking God to reveal and bring these into your life. Ask him for a plan

to govern your relationships until these personal confidants are released. Journal what he says.
4. Journal how you would handle a situation where a friend who you now lead was usurping your authority.

FIVEFOLD MINISTRY TIER TEAMS

1st Tier Foundational Vision Carriers
The core foundational team includes the main vision carriers. Everyone is not to be on this part of the team. This position is specifically chosen, identified and ordained by God. If people do not fit, do not force them as that is just a revealing that this is not where they are called as it relates to the vision.

I remember when I was considering my core vision carriers. I had in mind who those people would be. They were mature, equipped, claimed they were ready to walk in true fivefold ministry and had a heart for God and the things of God. God told me that these people were not my team. I was baffled because they fit my perception of what an equipped team member would be. But God showed me that even as that was so, they were not the team to carry the vision he had given me. That would soon be evident as most of them ended their relationship with me as I further aligned with the Lord. Only one couple stayed in my life and to this day, they still never became vision carriers. They are actually personal confidants, strong supports, intercessors, and advisors to my team and I.

When God revealed my team, I was "SHOOK." They were a group of young people who were still learning how to be faithful and accountable in their walk with him, had no ministry experience, and did not know anything about operating in their gifts, callings, or fivefold ministry. God said that as I empowered them as vision carriers, I would disciple them, train and equip them, and release them into their destiny, calling, and life's vision. God had me journal revelation that he provided concerning who they were to me personally, to the vision, what their destiny and calling was, and how it would impact the ministry vision and kingdom at large. He told me to have them pray about these areas, and then meet with them to confirm what he would reveal. I gave each person a month to receive direction from God. We then met and we confirmed each other's revelation regarding who they were as vision carriers. Let me take a moment to state the following regarding the process of developing and establishing vision carriers:

Some will be identified but will abort their position for various reasons:

- Some will be jealous of the other vision carriers and will not be able to SHIFT pass comparison and envy.
- Some will want the apostle/main leader all to themselves and this is impossible in fivefold ministry.
- Some will think they know better than the leader and engaging in usurping behaviors will abort their position.
- Some will be too busy comparing the ministry to previous experiences or other ministries. Altering or devaluing the leader and the vision will cause an abortion of their position.
- Some will not want to do the laborious work that comes with vision carrying. They will make life choices and decisions that may appear good, are permissive, but are not God's perfect will, thus altering and drawing them away from the ministry.
- Some may be exposed as opportunist or those familiar in relationship to the leader and the ministry, yet not innate vision carriers.
- Some will be out of timing and will need to return at a later season of the blueprint as God will be adamant about what is instilled in the foundation and he will not allow unyielded vision carriers to sow into the ministry vision.
- Some will be great, mature, sold out believers but are not God's ordained vision carriers of your blueprint.

The vision itself will expose and weed people out. The vision has a strategic blueprint and it will not SHIFT from the character, nature or identity of God for that blueprint. Anything that is not of God's design will present as contrary against God's original purpose for that vision. Even if it is a good concept or good person but not a God concept or a God ordained vision carrier, it will manifest in opposition to the vision. This is the reason Peter and Judas was exposed. The character and nature that was in them was contrary to the ministry vision. Peter was able to see his character flaws, make changes, and realign with the vision while Judas saw his character flaws, hated what he saw, could not get pass regret, and killed his own destiny (*Study Matthew 27, Luke 22, John 21-15-17*).

Jesus had twelve foundational vision carriers. The number you have is dependent on who God sends to assist in carrying the vision. Even if you discern ungodly or unhealthy things about them but God has called them to help carry the vision, be obedient with giving them a chance to transform into healthy vision carriers. However, guard the vision from any unhealthy seeds, fruit, and attacks they may potentially possess in harming the vision. Remember Jesus knew Judas would betray him, but Judas was still allowed every opportunity to SHIFT into his destiny. Yet, Jesus was not in denial about Judas' character and let him know that. You have to be honest with vision carriers so they can have an opportunity to change. Judas killed himself and his destiny because he did not heed to warning, nor did he pursue change. You will know ungodly vision carriers by their lack of response to turning away from ungodliness. It is okay to train them but do not expose the vision to their ungodliness.

The vision itself will expose and weed people out.

Judas betrayed Jesus but he could not infiltrate Jesus. SHIFT! SHIFT RIGHT NOW!

- Learn that when Jesus or your leader is revealing truth to you it is good. Denial delays transformation.
- Learn that exposure gives you the opportunity to SHIFT into the pure character, nature, and identity of God. Want what he wants for you.
- Learn to receive correction.
- Learn that constructive criticism is good.
- Do not allow poor choices to SHIFT you out of destiny!
- Learn to receive forgiveness and to forgive yourself.
- Learn to turn and to change.
- Be transformed so you can do destiny.
- Do not abort. Do not kill your own destiny by taking yourself out spiritually or naturally.
- Do not allow others to cause you to abort.
- Align, realign, and realign again when necessary.
- SHIFT RIGHT NOW!
- SHIFT!

2nd Tier Ministration Team
Moses in the Old Testament and the apostles in the New Testament had a ministration team (***Study Exodus 18, Acts 6***). These are vital vision carrying supports who use their gifts and callings to aide in completing extended duties that take a load off the 1st Tier team; while also helping

the ministry function smoothly and successfully. They are the body parts of the vision that keeps it and the 1st Tier team healthy, balanced, producing, reproducing, and multiplying the kingdom of God. As they assist with helping to make the vision operate smoothly, they should also be empowered, trained, and released in their own vision and calling which helps expand the body (*Study 1Corinthians 12:12-27*). Their ministration position provides hands on training where they can grow personally in their destiny, their calling and in activating the impartations and equipping they have received. As they demonstrate maturity, they should be encouraged to branch out further in what God is calling them to do to extend the work of the kingdom.

The 1st Tier team requires armorbearer assistants who aide with day to day personal and ministerial needs. The may come from the ministration team and may also be within the 1st Tier vision carrying team. Armorbearer assistants will be discussed in its own chapter. They are vital to helping to carry the vision of the ministry.

3rd Tier Apostolic Support Partners
These are support partners near and far that have the heart of God for the leader, team and ministry vision. God may also utilize them at times and for a season to assist with walking alongside the leader and the team in carrying and advancing the ministry vision. They have a heart for the 1st Tier team and the vision and recognize their role regarding it flourishing in the earth. They willingly give of their time, gifts, callings, resources, connections and finances to help build the vision. They intercede, war, mentor, coach, vision cast, serve, complete tasks, supply needs, sow financially and through blessings, partner in ministry, and etc. Be open to leaning on them and allowing them to be who God ordained them to be personally and ministerially to the team and vision.

4th Tier Event Team Members
The Events Team Members are those who help coordinate and fulfill tasks regarding events, (e.g. services, workshops, trainings, fellowships, etc.). They may or may not be members of the ministry. They may or may not be saved. They may provide food, clothing, gift bags, event materials, finances, connections, blessings, accommodations, aide with hosting, serving, media, operating equipment and anything else needed for events.

Mentoring and Equipping Team

This team includes those who will walk closely with helping to mentor, train and support the team and ministry. This team entails instructors who help to equip and build up the members and the ministry. They may be apostolic partners or invited ministers who come to impart into the members and the ministry. There may be a measure and even seasons of covenant with some of the ministers of the mentoring or equipping team, as this will be important in trusting members and the ministry to what they will impart.

Sojourners

I learned how to identity sojourners from Apostle Oscar Guobadia, founder of Brook Place Ministries in United Kingdom, London. Sojourners are seasonal and/or inconsistent people who the ministers and ministry will impart into from a posture of instructor, teacher, and/or revivalist. These people will come in and out of the ministry and out of the 1st Tier team's life to receive training and equipping from the ministry, while supporting at that time, but are not true vision carriers or members. It is important not to give sojourners positions or your heart as according to Apostle Oscar and my own personal experience, sojourners are vision partakers, not vision carriers. They can be given tasks and minor responsibilities, but not positions. They will not stay around and will leave the ministry and vision exposed if given positions. Sojourners may desire to commit and promise to commit but do not have the spiritual discipline to commit. They also may not be called to commit so the vision itself will expose them as sojourners and weed them out once they have gotten what they needed from the ministers and the ministries. It is important for the vision carriers and members to be clear and honest with themselves regarding the true purpose of sojourners and engage them from this place of truth. Apostle Oscar says it is important to "deal with them through their reality versus their potential." He contends *"a building cannot stand on potential as it is not physical material." "A building can only stand on physical material that is really there."*

Attendees

Attendees are people who attend and partake of your vision but are not invested in being part of the vision of the ministry. They may attend to receive encouragement, prayer, instruction, revelation, guidance on day to day situations, but are not seeking a destiny lifestyle or deep relationship with the members or the vision. Attendees are always good to have because you want to share the gospel of Jesus Christ with as many people as possible. You are also planting seeds that others can water at a later date.

> *1Corinthians 3:6 I planted, Apollos watered, but God gave the growth.*

It is important to recognize attendees, pour into them according to their needs and desires, but not give them roles of vision carriers and team members. They do not possess the dedication to be placed in these positions. Wait until they grow and desire more than just to attend, before giving them key roles in the vision. When they do volunteer, utilize them and encourage them to serve and minister more for God. This is also a form of planting seeds that can be watered as they continue to attend the ministry.

Infiltrators

Infiltrators are people that filter or permeate into your fivefold vision to gain access surreptitiously and gradually for personal gain, to acquire secret information, and for some malicious intent. They usually seek to join the team and willingly volunteer so they can have access to inside information regarding the leader and the vision. Some people are intentional infiltrators. Witches and warlocks will infiltrate ministries to gain access so they can cast spells against the ministry or sow discord to cause division and detriment to the vision. The enemy will send demonically oppressed people to infiltrate the ministry to gain control of certain parts of the vision, to influence and draw people away from the ministry, and to contaminate or cause challenges within the ministry. Sometimes severely soul wounded people that the ministry tries to help will turn out to be infiltrators. In your effort to help them, they will not want to do what it takes to process to wholeness. When they leave the ministry, they will use the access they had to the leader and the ministry in a slanderous manner. Because they are wounded and are operating through their wounds, they will twist information and experiences in effort to discredit the leader and the vision. Some people do not realize they are being used as infiltrators and you may not discern that they are infiltrators. Especially if they appear to have the heart of God, the character of the ministry, and understanding of the vision. They appear to want to be a part of what God is doing but there is some underlying motive that will subtly show itself as they will become divisive against the order, structure, authority, or protocol of the vision. They will begin to usurp authority, make subtle inferences regarding how matters are conducted within the ministry, or challenge the belief system of the leader and the ministry with false, erred, or ungodly doctrine or revelation. When corrected, they will become offended and seek to rally others that they have influenced to prove their case against the leader and the ministry. If this proves unsuccessful, they will leave the ministry, and often become publicly slanderous against the leader and the vision. Infiltrators must be addressed and exposed immediately when they are discerned. And any misguidance and ungodly revelation or doctrine they have sown into the people and vision must be rectified. Otherwise, it will continue to mature in the people and the vision and further sow malice and error.

> *Jude 1:4 For there are certain men crept in unawares, who were before of old ordained to this condemnation, ungodly men, turning the grace of our God into lasciviousness, and denying the only Lord God, and our Lord Jesus Christ.*

> *2Timothy 3:4-7 Traitors, heady, high minded, lovers of pleasures more than lovers of God; Having a form of godliness, but denying the power thereof: from such turn away. For of this sort are they which creep into houses, and lead captive silly women laden with sins, led away with divers lusts, Ever learning, and never able to come to the knowledge of the truth. Now as Jannes and Jambres withstood Moses, so do these also resist the truth: men of corrupt minds, reprobate concerning the faith. But they shall proceed no further: for their folly shall be manifest unto all men, as their's also was.*

> *Titus 1:10-16 For there are many unruly and vain talkers and deceivers, specially they of the circumcision: Whose mouths must be stopped, who subvert whole houses, teaching things which they ought not, for filthy lucre's sake. One of themselves, even a prophet of their own, said, the Cretians are always liars, evil beasts, slow bellies. This witness is true. Wherefore rebuke them sharply, that they may be sound in the faith; Not giving heed to Jewish fables, and commandments of men, that turn from the truth. Unto the pure all things are pure: but unto them that are defiled and unbelieving is nothing pure; but even their mind and conscience is defiled. They profess that they know God; but in works they deny him, being abominable, and disobedient, and unto every good work reprobate.*

> *2Peter 2:1-3 But there were false prophets also among the people, even as there shall be false teachers among you, who privily shall bring in damnable heresies, even denying the Lord that bought them, and bring*

upon themselves swift destruction. And many shall follow their pernicious ways; by reason of whom the way of truth shall be evil spoken of. And through covetousness shall they with feigned words make merchandise of you: whose judgment now of a long time lingereth not, and their damnation slumbereth not.

2Peter 2:10 *But chiefly them that walk after the flesh in the lust of uncleanness, and despise government. Presumptuous are they, self willed, they are not afraid to speak evil of dignities.*

The Amplified Bible *And especially [d]those who indulge in the corrupt passions of the sin nature, and despise authority. Presumptuous and reckless, self-willed and arrogant [creatures, despising the majesty of the Lord], they do not tremble when they revile angelic majesties.*

Homework Explorations:

1. Study the story of Peter denying Jesus and Judas betraying Jesus in ***Matthew 27, Luke 22, John 21-15-17***, and journal revelation God gives you about their character and how to be conscious of their operations.
2. Journal how you would handle the Peters' and Judas' as they come to your ministry.
3. Study ***Exodus 18*** and ***Acts 6.*** Journal what you learned about a ministration team.
4. Study ***1Corinthians 12:12-27***. Journal what revelation God gives you regarding us being one body with different members. Journal revelation that will be helpful to implement into the ministry vision you are part of.
5. Study ***2Peter 2***. Journal your revelation regarding his chapter. Journal what you learned about infiltrators and seek God for biblical insight on how to discern them. Journal what he reveals.
6. Seek God for five insights on how to identify a main vision carrier in your ministry. Journal what he shares.

BUILDING A FIVEFOLD MINISTRY CULTURE

Acts 2:42-47 And they continued stedfastly in the apostles' doctrine and fellowship, and in breaking of bread, and in prayers. And fear came upon every soul: and many wonders and signs were done by the apostles. And all that believed were together, and had all things common; And sold their possessions and goods, and parted them to all men, as every man had need. And they, continuing daily with one accord in the temple, and breaking bread from house to house, did eat their meat with gladness and singleness of heart, Praising God, and having favour with all the people. And the Lord added to the church daily such as should be saved.

In this passage of scripture, we have the true representation of a fivefold ministry culture occurring among a body of believers. The word says they were engaged in steadfastness in the apostles' doctrine and fellowship. They were operating in continual perseverance, diligence, devotion, in teaching, instruction, and assembling together in commune of fivefold ministry. They were constantly studying the word, training and equipping themselves in the destinies and visions God had given them.

Hebrew words for *fellowship* is *koinonia* and means:
1. fellowship, association, distribution, community, communion, joint participation, intercourse
2. the share which one has in anything, participation intercourse, fellowship, intimacy
3. the right hand as a sign and pledge of fellowship (in fulfilling the apostolic office)
4. a gift jointly contributed, a collection, a contribution, as exhibiting an embodiment and proof of fellowship breaking bread

This was a close knit body of believers. So close that it was likened unto intercourse and intimacy. This means they were consciously invested in one another's lives and in the ministry vision. They were committed to being jointly connected and to flow together where they embodied one another in everything that they did.

I want to make sidebar comment and say that many contend they want this type of interaction and fellowship in a ministry, and boast that this is what ministry should look like. But when they get it – see it - when they realize folks is all up in their face, their business, their lives, in their houses, their sins - they are challenged. It takes real commitment, submission and vulnerability to create this type of culture and to receive it as a lifestyle. It also requires responsibility and accountability as what is taking place is covenant. Intimacy is a covenant act. We do not realize that ministry is an intimate exchange with God and with one another. Anyone who has a challenge with this level of covenant responsibility and accountability, wants to have intercourse by engaging God and the body of Christ in deep spiritual and soulish acts that are very personal to God, and then get up like there was not a soul and spiritual exchange taking place. Yet, it is the illustration of true fivefold ministry.

This fivefold ministry continually prayed together, feasted and took the Lord's supper together. They were persistent and intentional in the culture of unity, building one another up and growing together that they were creating. There was such a one ness that a reverential fear came upon every soul. Not some but EVERY SOUL! MY GOD! That word fear means *"fright, terror, dread, reverence."* Can you imagine every soul in your ministry fearing God with immeasurable reverence and awe? Wanting him and what he is doing so bad that they feared not being fervent in the things of the Lord? Being SHIFTED into such a devout and dutiful drive for God and the ministry until they dreaded – were afraid of – not communing daily with him and other believers? This created an open heaven where signs and wonders became commonplace. These are the benefits we do not discern when an effort to create such a ministry culture occurs. We do not realize that constant communing, prayer, breaking bed, and a lifestyle of worshipful devotion to God, produces an atmosphere for consistent miracles, signs, and wonders. SHIFT RIGHT NOW! SHIFT!

> *One fact I experienced about fivefold ministry is that everything about your life at some point becomes part of the vision.*

I want to sidebar again and state that when leaders strive to create this type of culture, those who did not SHIFT into a reverential fear of the Lord, or onlookers who fear intimacy, will label it a cult. They attempt to quench the dedication, excitement, and honor of those who have yielded to the full vision of fivefold ministry, and who are now responding to its impact on their lives, posture to God, and those they are in covenant with. I do want to encourage you that as you SHIFT into fivefold ministry, and

God releases covenant relationships and fellowship to you, never let people talk you out of the good thing you have going with God and his people. Why would you let someone who cannot offer anything steal fulfillment from you? Why would you let someone who has not even experienced what you have with God and those he has put in your life, speak ill of it, while also encouraging you to separate from it? Be watchful of these sabotage spirits – covenant breaker (divorce). They are not for you. They are just unhappy so they want you to be too. But I digress. Again we are talking about the culture of true fivefold ministry. SHIFT!

The word says, *"And all that believed were together, and had all things common."* I JUST SHOUTED! I did a SHIFT move. MY GOD! This demonstrates the clarity they had about the fivefold ministry vision and their ability to pick it up and run with it. But the key was that they believed in the vision God had given – that the apostles conveyed. I must sidebar. I know so many people who attend church and even those that are fivefold, yet do not fully believe in the vision of the ministry. They quest it, the leadership, the promises and prophecies of God. Yet, they wonder why the fullness of the vision does not flourish. Disbelief is actually an atheist or anti-Christ posture. Disbelief therefore stifles progress. If disbelief is part of the culture, then the environment will produce an anti-Christ climate. You must be all in if you want to see the fruit of the vision manifest. You must be in agreement with those you are fellowshipping with and have ALL things in common with them. ALL THINGS! SHIFT RIGHT NOW! SHIFT

This fivefold ministry was so in tune with one another that they were self-sacrificing. They willingly sold their possessions and goods – their land, estates, movable goods – then distributed the wealth to make sure all had what they needed. WHEWWWW! Work on me Lord! I remember when God told me to begin having services in my home. I had already given up and sacrificed so much for ministry. I was SOOOOOOO SHOOK by this because it was my one solace that was my own. The more services I had, the more self-sacrificing I had to become. The ministry items were in every room, closet, and corner of my home. I was a neat freak so keeping everything to my standards was a job in and of itself. Initially, there would be days where I had to repent for feeling like nothing was mines anymore, and ask God to give me a joyful heart and a selfless nature about all the sacrifices I was making. Eventually, I had to assert my right to have something for myself because I was so freely giving. The voice, revelation, glory, acceleration, signs and wonders of God were definitely evident. People did not want to go home because of what they were experiencing. We never seemed to know how to end services because of how God would invade us. But that was not what SHIFTED my posture, as one fact I experienced about fivefold ministry is that everything about your life at some point becomes part of the vision. Even if it is just for a season. There will be an innate drawing in you that will want to sacrifice to support the vision in advancing. You will want to sacrifice for others so that they can be successful in the vision. I believe this resurrects from Jesus being the cornerstone of the vision. Jesus was the ultimate sacrifice. He gave his life that all would be saved. When you start to cultivate a fivefold culture where he is the center, it just yields you to be sacrificing. I also want to state that at some point a SHIFT takes place inside your spirit where all you want is what God is doing and you have an unwavering trust that nothing is to be compared to what is occurring and to come as you are obedient and steadfast in him. People will see your sacrifice and think it is too much. I have had people reject my walk and ministry because they do not want to sacrifice or to endure what I have experienced. They do not realize the fruit it bears and that what they are really seeing is the nature of Jesus manifesting in me. Which is what we all should be doing – representing Jesus.

This fivefold ministry had SHIFTED into a place of selfless covenant with God and with one another. Their fivefold ministry was mobile as they went from house to house releasing the vision. This means that families and households were also being transformed and cultivated in their fivefold ministry culture. They were praising and worshipping, preaching, and eating in oneness of heartfelt joy. The community received and favored them. They experienced revival reformation as people were saved and added to the ministry daily. Fivefold ministry should not only impact those that are a part of the vision, but also the people in the community and the region. People should be drawn to God and to the vision because of what they witness God doing. It should not be a downtrodden gospel, but an exuberant celebration of life like they saw in this body of believers.

I am praying that this SHIFT occurs in you and spreads contagiously as you cultivate your fivefold ministry culture. I do believe that because of church hurt, fallen leaders, misunderstandings about the church, and the assault against the church in this day and time, we have our work cut out for us and require some skills building in effort to cultivate a true fivefold ministry environment. I have had to teach my team relationship skills, communication and conflict resolution skills, social and interpersonal skills, how to respect one another's process, the art of true covenant, and on and on to assist with cultivating a loving, self-sacrificing fivefold ministry environment. I have had to practice this daily with them and teach it just as strongly as I have the Bible, their destiny and calling. One of the main challenges we have had is people coming into the ministry and being overwhelmed by the love, level of sacrifice, purity, sold out mindset, wholeness, spirit of excellence and expectation of wellness that radiates from us and the vision. Many do not honor the process and comparing themselves to us or being envious, often causes them to abort because the fruit of what has been cultivated takes root in them. I am sharing this not to discourage you as this Acts 2 culture is possible. We live it. We are now learning how to draw people into it and solidify them in it. I shared that to say that it will take work and as a vision carrier, you will have to want to do the work. I am loving the fruit of the work we have been doing in our ministry vision and I know you will find it is possible and worth it too.

In the next chapter, I provide some applicable tools and revelations to assist in this area. They are key to our breakthrough and will be key to yours. Thanking God for your fivefold ministry culture even now. SHIFT!

Homework Explorations:
1. Journal your revelations concerning this chapter.
2. Seek God for what your fivefold ministry culture should look like. Journal what he says.
3. Journal what you will need to implement and the sacrifices you and your team will need to make to create the culture God is requiring.
4. Begin to practice cultivating yourself, your team, and your environment daily to help manifest your fivefold ministry culture.

HEALTHY RELATIONSHIP NUGGETS

Some of this chapter is from Dr. Taquetta Baker's book, "Healing The Wounded Leader

Learning One Another's Personalities Types

Everyone has different personality types that are generally defined by our identity, calling, upbringing, experiences, ethnicity, belief systems, etc. It will be important for vision carriers, team members, and members of the ministry to take the time to learn and value one another's personality types, and to have grace as people SHIFT out of ungodly behavioral characteristics into godly ones.

Consistent team and ministry building activities, fellowship, and talking about one another's life experiences, likes, dislikes, desires, goals, aspirations, etc., is key to learning one another's personality types. This is especially important for the foundational vision carriers as how they interact is instilled into the foundation of the vision and thus cultivated into the ministry. I believe it is important for the main vision carrier to have a personal relationship with all vision carriers so they can learn their personality and how they operate. Also while vision casting, it is important to share with the team what your personality type is like so they will know what to expect from you. You will be surprised how this will help diminish offense, psychological and mental warfare. As when people know how you are, they are less likely to be offended by certain things you do that are not intended to be offensive or challenging but may come across that way.

There are some attributes such as pet peeves, unhealthy behaviors and characteristics that will need to be cleansed and gutted out of the personalities of all members because they are not God. Just because we may be challenged by certain matters and have had certain experiences in our lives, does not mean we are justified in behaving ungodly or carrying certain mindsets. It is the responsibility of the main vision carrier, designated mentors and counselors to correct and reprove ungodly behaviors and attributes in believers and to teach them applicable tools for healthy behavior and interaction. It will be important for believers to be willing to work on these issues and not want to keep them. Strive to want to have the character and nature of Jesus and to represent him. Holding on to pet peeves and ungodly behaviors opens the door to sin and offense toward others. Maturity is about being more like Christ so you can build others up in the love and empowerment of Christ. I decree this will be the desired posture of every vision carrier and member of your fivefold ministry. SHIFT RIGHT NOW! SHIFT!

Respecting One Another's Growth Process
Everyone in the ministry will grow and mature at different paces depending on the calling on their lives, the generational legacy they are a part of, the personal cultivation, the training, equipping, impartations, promises and prophecies they have received, the seasons of acceleration, and their drive and cultivation of personal relationship with God. It will be important to respect where one another are in your personal walks, resist comparison, jealousy and envy, and create a culture of continuously honoring and empowering one another. The enemy will come for your unity through this avenue. He will seek to cause division, strife, unworthiness, rejection, insecurity, sabotage, destiny murder, etc., by having your focus on where others are in comparison to your own journey. It will be important for vision carriers and leaders to have grace in relations to the growth process of those they oversee. This will aid in not becoming frustrated, grieved, sharp with the tongue and weary, where you mishandle members because you are challenged by their process. There will be times where your challenges may be justified, but this will come through a well of righteous indignation and having the heart of God for that person's destiny, more so than your soulish or emotion realm. Check with God so you will know exactly where your feelings are deriving from and deal with them accordingly. Ask God to give you his eyes for those you do ministry with and oversee, and cultivate this focus as a foundational ministry attribute. This will also aid in not operating in unhealthy judgments and offenses as you journey in life and ministry with vision carriers and members.

Interpersonal Skills & Social Skills
Teaching your vision carriers and members these skills aide them in learning qualities and behaviors that are essential to interacting with others in a positive and proper manner. These skills are important as people are coming into your ministry and business with relationship dynamics that they learned from their families, upbringings and experiences. They are shaped by these environments and will need to be transformed by the skills and patterns of the Lord. It is important not to assume that they will automatically incur these skills by becoming saved. These skills must be taught and role modeled. And each member should be held accountable for implementing them. This is also important as we

live in a time where everyone is pursuing happiness, and the boundaries are blurred on what is appropriate. Godly interactions are important and how people care for one another's hearts and souls is vital to having a healthy ministry environment. Have counselors and consultants come in and train in these areas and require all members to practice them as a lifestyle. The more this becomes your culture, the easier it will be for new members to succumb to the climate you are planting.

Boundaries
Boundaries are vital for a leader/member relationship. Boundaries must be clear and explicit. They should not cross sexual lines. Neither person should get needs and desires met that are beyond the scope of the covenant God is requiring for the relationship.
People can only fulfill the roles in your life that God designed. Moreover, people have choices, so they can decide what role they will play in your life. Fulfilling roles that God did not ordain provokes expectations that will breech boundaries, thus causing wounds and drama in the relationship and ministry.

No matter how much you try to make a person be more and try to acquire more from them, God's will and their choice, will override your desires. As a result, you will be left wanting, longing, frustrated, in drama, spewing drama and feeling rejected.

Seek healing when you find yourself wanting and pursuing more from someone than God, or the person is willing to give.

Instead of seeking people and trying to receive fulfillment from them, seek God as he can be everything you need. He can also connect you in the right timing to balanced relationships that can bring fulfillment to your life.

Anytime you are so focused on what people cannot and will not be to you, you miss the value of what they can be. You also miss the revelation that they were not meant to fulfill that need or desire in your life.

It is important to let people know what your needs, desires and expectations are. Otherwise, you are having one relationship with the person in your head, in your fantasies, and a whole other one in real life. When you do this, it causes drama, conflict, discouragement and can wreck the relationship you are to have with the person. It is usually you who is behaving this way, while blaming your broken heart on the person rather than on your inability to effectively communicate your needs, desires, and expectations.

Healthy Communication & Conflict Resolution Skills

Learn healthy communication and conflict resolution skills, and role model and teach others how to communicate and resolve conflict. Interrogation is when forceful, threatening, battering questions and statements are used to obtain information. Interrogation is not communication. It puts people on the defense and guard where they do not feel comfortable or safe to share information. It also causes people to feel pressured to share information or agree with statements that may not necessarily be the truth or their truth. Such communication should be avoided in godly settings as it comes across as controlling and manipulative.

Conflict does not mean disconnect or divorce. It just means all parties involved have a challenge to work through and that is okay. Challenges teach us a lot about one another and enable us to take the relationship to a deeper dimension of unconditional love, forgiveness, patience, godly character, and grace as they process and mature personally and in relationship regarding who each person is individually and to one another. Do not be afraid of conflict. Learn to embrace it as part of life and relationships. The key is learning how to communicate and resolve conflict in a biblical healthy manner. The biblical applicable keys below will bless you, however, my *"Annihilating The Powers Of Church Hurt"* has a detailed chapter on biblically examining and resolving conflict.

1. Stay focused and listen attentively.
2. Ask open ended questions rather than closed ended questions that put people on the defense.
3. Do not attack. Express that these are your thoughts and feelings and allow the person a chance to explain themselves. Encourage them to give you the same opportunity. "I" statements are good because you are expressing how you perceived the situation without outright attacking or blaming. This is beneficial in instances where misperceptions have occurred.
4. Repeat what you need clarity on so the person can correct or elaborate on what they said. Remember, clarity brings knowledge and knowledge is power.

5. Be okay with conflict and disagreement; it is what makes us unique. When you embrace conflict as a part of healthy communication, you will resolve conflict quicker and easier.
6. Stay focused on resolving the matter and not allowing challenging thoughts and emotions to shut down the conversation.
7. Emotions and challenging thoughts are going to arise. But they should not rule your ability to be tempered, meek and articulate. Focus on communicating through your spirit and the character of God rather than your emotions.
8. Be conscious with talking to God in your mind. Ask him to speak through you and to guide you in your responses.
9. Be honest and express your thoughts, feelings, concerns and disagreements in a calm and respectful manner.
10. Pay attention to nonverbal communication and undertones. Be open to addressing these forms of communication.
11. Be discerning when the conversation stops being about you and the person and SHIFTS to exposing unresolved issues. This happens a lot in leader/member relationships. Leaders are often a catalyst for healing mother, father, teacher and authority figure wounds.
12. After resolving challenging situations, engage in small talk to restore joy, peace and ease within the relationship interactions.
13. Start and end meetings and conflicts with prayer. Forgive where necessary, cleanse out hurtful feelings and thoughts; restore trust, honor, love and validation one to another.
14. Do not take phone calls or texts unless it is an emergency.

The inability to communicate your needs, thoughts, desires and motives, is the result of a deeper issue. Even if you were not taught or role modeled healthy and effective communication, you are mature enough to stop using your upbringing and past as an excuse. Deal with your underlying root issues while receiving deliverance and healing. You are also mature enough to learn the tools needed to communicate your thoughts, feelings and motives in a healthy manner.

Stop engaging in the generational and relational cycle that makes you broken and unhealthy. Do not let people draw you into generational and relational cycles that God has delivered you from.

The only person that can bring value to your words, thoughts and feelings is you. If you cannot express them, do not expect anyone else to give them a voice or value them.

Nuggets For Receiving Constructive Criticism

Learn to view correction, rebuke and constructive criticism as the love and protection of God.

> ***Proverbs 29:15*** *The rod and reproof give wisdom: but a child left [to himself] bringeth his mother to shame.*

> ***Revelation 3:19*** *As many as I love, I rebuke and chasten: be zealous therefore, and repent.*

> ***Hebrews 4:12*** *For the word of God [is] quick, and powerful, and sharper than any twoedged sword, piercing even to the dividing asunder of soul and spirit, and of the joints and marrow, and [is] a discerner of the thoughts and intents of the heart.*

> ***Hebrews 12:7-8*** *If ye endure chastening, God dealeth with you as with sons; for what son is he whom the father chasteneth not? But if ye be without chastisement, whereof all are partakers, then are ye bastards, and not sons.*

<u>Chastening is *paideia* in Greek</u> and means:
1. tutorage, i.e. education or training; by implication, disciplinary correction: — chastening, chastisement, instruction, nurture
2. the whole training and education of children (which relates to the cultivation of mind and morals, and employs for this purpose now commands and admonitions, now reproof and punishment)
3. It also includes the training and care of the body, whatever is in adults also cultivates the soul, esp. by correcting mistakes and curbing passions
4. instruction which aims at increasing virtue chastisement
5. chastening, (of the evils with which God visits men for their amendment)

   - Chastening is not just about correcting. It is about instructing, training, educating, nurturing, caring, restoring, enlightening, cultivating, empowering and bringing discipline and sustainable consistency to a person's journey of sonship with

the Lord. Members must see the purpose of correction and constructive criticism as it keeps them safe, progressing and journeying in the truth and wellness of the Lord.
- When constructive criticism is given listen attentively. Focus with your spirit and strive to fully comprehend the feedback provided.
- If you do not fully understand, ask for clarity.
- Take notes so you can refer to what was being spoken and seek God for further revelation on how to implement the revelation to bring about change.
- Set measurable goals that can help you discern your improvement.
- After a specific amount of time seek feedback regarding your transformation and what other improvements may be necessary for your growth and development.
- If you disagree with the correction, rebuke, or constructive criticism, share that in a respectful manner. Ask what exactly is being expected of you and seek to explore what may be lost in translation. Have a posture that the person providing feedback has your best interest at heart and the heart of God for you so you can seek to hear through your spirit and not offense. Make sure your disagreement is not coming from a wound, insecurity, unworthiness, pride, perfectionism, an inability to search yourself, rebellion, or anti-submissiveness. Deal with these attributes in your private prayer time with the Lord so accepting feedback can be a positive experience. Be cognizant not to make excuses for poor behavior and sins. The more you justify wrongdoings, the more difficult it is to receive feedback.
- Be patient by taking the information before the Lord first before you rebut it. Examine yourself before him and be honest about what he shows you. If you still are not seeing where the feedback was from him, seek further dialog regarding the matter. Sometimes strongholds can prevent you from receiving feedback. Sometimes it is best to implement what has been suggested and allow your actions to break down the strongholds where you can discern truth concerning a matter. This requires being open to submitting to your leader and those God has put over you, and trusting the wisdom he gives them to mature your life.

Hebrews 13:17 *Obey them that have the rule over you, and submit yourselves: for they watch for your souls, as they that must give account, that they may do it with joy, and not with grief: for that is unprofitable for you.*

Nuggets For Giving Correction, Rebuke & Constructive Criticism

1. I suggest to have another vision carrier present when meeting with members.
2. When meeting with the opposite sex, have another vision carrier present.
3. It would be beneficial to tape all meetings and give it to the person to search out with the Lord as they seek to apply what has been discussed. This also can aid in situations with people who do not know how to express their feelings in a healthy manner and are who are striving to cause challenges for members or the ministry.
4. Pray and seek God regarding what to share and how to share it.
5. Cleanse any offense, judgments, frustrations and weariness regarding the person or issue at hand.
6. Ask for God's eyes, love and heart for the person and ask him to make sure it is tangible in your interactions with the person.
7. Seek the wise counsel of your overseer for difficult situations that require more strategic wisdom and revelation.
8. When meeting with the person, share positive feedback, strengths, growths and any ways the person has been striving to improve and work on matters.
9. Share regarding the challenges at hand and how improving would benefit the person personally, their relationship with God, and the ministry.
10. Do not attack the person, but share in a way where dialog can be twofold.
11. If the discussion is becoming heated where anger or offense is stirring, take a moment to pray and cleanse these attributes. If this does not work, consider canceling the meeting then having it another day when both parties can express their thoughts and feelings in a healthy manner.

12. Give them an opportunity to share their perception about the feedback and provide further insight, wisdom, correction and constructive criticism as needed.
13. Make sure your feedback is specific. Try not to bring up old situations unless you are addressing a cycle or pattern that needs to be exposed. Otherwise, stay present focused and offer solutions for transformation.
14. Set measurable goals that the person can work on and set a time for them to demonstrate improvement.
15. Set a follow up meeting to discuss progress and any further improvement needed.
16. If the person requires greater clarity and does not seem to be accepting the feedback, try giving further feedback to help them understand. If there seems to be a blockage, encourage them to pray into what was discussed and then share with you what God speaks to them.
17. If they still do not receive after searching with God, encourage them to trust your feedback and allow their willingness to work on what was suggested to breakdown strongholds that may be hindering them from receiving. As they come into revelation, encourage them to be honest and share with you the understanding they have gained.
18. Praise them for changes you see in them to promote further growth and maturity.

Check Your Desires

If you are driven by your need for love and belonging, where your desires are not put in check/right perspective, please know they will show in your interactions with your friends, acquaintances, and members. You will be possessive, jealous, comparing your interactions with that person to what they do with others, resentful, self-rejecting, then sulking when someone inquires as to the reason you have isolated yourself. And even when you try to physically get close to that person, they will feel uncomfortable because though it should be a hug, holding of the hand, laying on the shoulder or lap, etc., they can feel your inappropriate desires in what should be a genuine pure interaction.

When we are getting our need for love and belonging met outside of God's presence, it generally leaves us wanting, longing and broken. Seek God to heal areas of inadequacy, worth, identity, and unresolved relationship issues, while letting him bring and guide you to fulfillment in these areas of your life.

We all have an innate need for love and belonging, but when we are driven by it, it is lust that is guiding us.

When people cannot, will not, or should not fulfill needs, desires and expectations that you have, respect these boundaries and choices. Ask God to cleanse you of any unhealthy or imbalanced soulties or emotions you have for the person. This is important because it does not matter if you stalk people in your mind or in real life; they have a choice to connect with you or not. We set ourselves up for self-rejection when we try to make people be what they are not to be or do not want to be in our lives.

Members will want to be close to you because you are the leader. It is important to have your desires in check so you will not overstep boundaries and engage in interactions that could lend you and others to sin.

Mind Stalking
Mind stalking is when you have an entire relationship in your mind with someone and in reality it is totally different. This is just as dangerous and scary as physically stalking someone, and even more so because usually stalkers are not allowed in a person's vicinity or personal space yet desires to be. A mind stalker is usually in the person's circle, but desires to be more to the person than what they are. They can be a friend, acquaintance, companion, or team member who wants to be closer to you than what they are.

Unbeknown to the person, the mind stalker is usually engaging with the person through his or her desires and motives, or through jealousy, anger, rejection, and resentment due to not being able to have what they want from that person. By the time the person figures it out, they are caught up in drama, confusion, and no longer trusting their judgment of people.

Leaders will have a few encounters with mind stalkers. Boundaries are essential with mind stalkers. The minute you make them more or give them more information about you than you should have, you have fed their desire and made them think they are important to you. As you balance this, they may become blatantly aggressive or passive aggressive, but they will make sure you know they are offended. It is best to have meetings with them with third parties present. And to have public conversations where others can be witnesses of the interactions. Many mind stalkers are unstable and unpredictable, so it is always better to keep yourself safe and accountable regardless to what they are thinking, may say, or may do.

Self-Rejection
Self-rejection will have you pushing people away and calling it the Lord. You will have a plethora of reasons as to why they cannot be in your life. Much of it is because people cannot be what you want, or you lack being able to truly connect to who they can be to you. And some of it is because you want people to be perfect cause you fear being hurt, so your focus is on who they are not, rather than who they can be.

Some self-rejection is because we want people to be God. We are looking for a redeemer, a healer, and someone who can fulfill our every need. Only God can do that sir/ma'am! Interestingly, the self-rejector rejects God, even when he is beckoning to be what they need.

Some members will reject your fellowship and leadership, then contend you are not adequately governing their soul. They need deliverance from self-rejection, and until they are delivered, they will not be able to receive from you or any other leader. Be cognizant of not getting so caught up in validating these people that it drains you. Instead, spend time interceding for them and assign them a counselor or mentor that can walk with them to wholeness. As they are healed, they will begin to engage you, and then you can begin investing time into developing a healthy relationship with them.

Foolish Relationships
> ***Proverbs 13:20*** *He that walketh with wise men shall be wise: but a companion of fools shall be destroyed.*

A fool is a stupid, insensitive, arrogant person, a silly person; a person who lacks judgment or sense. A fool is an ardent enthusiast who cannot resist an opportunity to indulge in enthusiasm. That means they will spend and sell your heart at the expense of their own self-indulgence. While you are hurting, they will think it is funny, or find it pleasing to have gotten over on you.

A fool is also a weak-minded or idiotic person. So when you befriend or remain in relationship with a fool, you are setting yourself up to be deteriorated as a person, and to even be destroyed by their ignorance and folly. Stop blaming them. You have choices. Cut ties, heal and move on.

Foolish relationships are draining, drama filled, and can destroy whatever joy or focus you have at the time. As a leader you are not obligated to entertain such relationships. Do not be someone else's emotional roller coaster as this is not Godly, or a requirement as a soul watcher. Lead the person from the context of a congregational relationship and let that be that. You are giving them what they can handle at the time, and until they are willing to learn by practicing healthy relationship dynamics, you are not obligated by God to waste your time.

Foolish Relationships Cause Eternal Scars
> ***Proverbs 13:20*** *He that walketh with wise men shall be wise: but a companion of fools shall be destroyed.*

<u>*Destroyed*</u> in Hebrew is *mar* and means:
1. especially by breaking; figuratively, to split the ears (with sound), i.e. Shout (for alarm or joy)
2. blow an alarm, cry (alarm, aloud, out), destroy
3. make a joyful noise, smart, shout (for joy), sound an alarm, triumph

There is indeed an alarm going off when we are engaged in relationships with unhealthy people. These people are seeking to triumph over us. Our destruction is their victory, as all kinds of alarms are going off within the relationship to let us know they are not healthy for us. Mar actually means to disfigure, scar, deface, render less perfect. A stripping of our identity occurs when we are in relationships with foolish people. We become unrecognizable at the expense of their personal gain. They truly turn us into people that we were never meant to be, and cause us to settle for less than what we should have in life.

When a disfiguring occurs, it is difficult to get back to your original self without having a scar or something to remind you that a change occurred. Even as you heal, your heart, soul, and physical disposition will never be the same. Foolish relationships are not worth such scars. Get out while you can, and be wise not to enter into them altogether.

Some Relationships Cannot be Fixed
> ***Proverbs 13:20*** *He that walketh with wise men shall be wise: but a companion of fools shall be destroyed.*

God calls relationships with fools unwise. That means no matter how much you try to stay and fix the relationship or the person, you are fooling yourself because the only wise thing to do is to get out of the relationship altogether. You cannot fix what was never meant to be - what was doomed for destruction from the beginning. Some people will come under your ministry, and relationships will either never gel or will be breeched such that they are unfixable. God will give you peace and clarity when such relationships surface. Follow his leading and trust what he is saying. He is saving you from unnecessary drama and wounds.

Unhealthy Relationships Imprison the Soul
Sometimes we are not willing or do not have the strength to release unhealthy relationships because of soulties that attach us to the person. Our soul could also be imprisoned to the person. ***Proverbs 22:24-25*** speaks of the snared soul. It reads, "Make no friendship with an angry man; and with a furious man thou shalt not go: Lest thou learn his ways, and get a snare to thy soul."

Though this scripture uses the word angry, that word angry also means a person who causes long suffering or an ire person. So if you are in a relationship with a person that causes you suffering or ire which means an unhealthy intense passion where there is always drama, chaos, wrath or conflict, and you are having a difficult time releasing this relationship, it could be because your soul is snared.

Snare means "to trap, hook, capture, entangled."

As you remain in an unhealthy relationship, your soul becomes a prisoner of that person. You are striving to learn their ways so you will not set them off, but your soul is already ensnared by their wrath, because they are dictating and controlling your life with their moods, drama, unhealthy entanglements and actions.

To be free, you have to break soulties with these people, and command your soul to be free from their imprisonment. Bondages of fear, control, confusion, bewitchment and word curses also have to be broken off your life, and any deposits of them need to be cleansed out of your soul. Fall out of agreement with feeling like you need this person and cannot live without them and are obligated to have relationship with them. Break any words and deeds that have been released over you in this manner.

A lot of times, we do not want to let relationships go because we feel like a failure, feel rejected, stuck in familiarity, or have some type of false loyalty or obligation to the person we are holding on to, or to our position as a leader. Yet, no one should be abusing you and in no way should you feel ensnared where you are having to dictate and maneuver around people's actions. ***Proverbs 27:17*** tells us that "*Iron sharpens iron, so a man sharpeneth the countenance of his friend.*"

Even though you are the leader, those under you should still be sharpening you in some measure. When being sharpened you are being empowered to be the best you that you can be. If there is a cutting away of who you are, it is only to perfect the essence of who you are in a greater measure. You should always become a better you through those you are in relationship with. If you become less and even stagnant where you are no longer growing and being empowered to grow, then the relationship should be reevaluated. Either you all are not being who you are to be to one another, or you are holding on to the relationship for other reasons that have no true defined divine purpose. Be okay with letting go and allowing God to connect you in relationships that can sharpen you.

> ***The Message Bible*** *You use steel to sharpen steel, and one friend sharpens another.*

The Victim Mentality
Sometimes people are not healed from past hurts. They are not able to receive constructive criticism or personal examination that promotes Godly transformation. Anytime someone speaks truth to them, they feel hurt and victimized. Their past wounds cause them to misinterpret correction, rebuke, or enlightenment regarding a challenging matter, and assume they are being abused and victimized when that is not the case. They SHIFT deeper into living through their wounds and offense. Be mindful of the victim mentality and help people to get delivered from it. Teach them healthy skills so they will know how to communicate, resolve conflict, engage in healthy relationship and social interactions, receive correction, rebuke and constructive criticism.

Relationship Empowerment

Proverbs 27:17 tells us that *"Iron sharpens iron, so a man sharpeneth the countenance of his friend."* Iron is sharpened by rubbing it against another piece of sharp iron. When two pieces of iron, especially iron blades rub together, both become sharper. Also an equipping is occurring as both are empowering the other through the connection they have with one another. Both begin to change and transform while becoming more refined. Each are then more efficient for use.

Sharp means *"to become keen, acute, alert, watchful, defined, cutting edge, swift, tapered, fierce."*

When people do not sharpen one another, the relationship becomes dull, slow, lazy, un-useful and blurred in vision. Feelings are easily hurt due to unspoken and unmet expectations flaring. These expectations tend to out way the level of iron production manifesting in the relationship. If the relationship is unfruitful or not beneficial, check the iron production. For whatever reason, either you or the other person is not investing in the relationship. Someone has to start sharpening the other for production to manifest, so if you are waiting on the other person, you are already demonstrating that you have some issues with investing in relationships or in that person.

Examine yourself and that relationship, and be okay with releasing it if necessary or doing what is necessary to sharpen it so it can produce what God has required of it.

If people are not growing under your ministry, connect them with ministries that can sharpen them. Give them your blessing if they feel they have received all they can from your ministry and desire to move on where they can be sharpened. If it was not time for them to go, God will deal with them and even have them return to further be sharpened under your ministry.

Homework Explorations:

1. Journal your experiences with four of these relationship challenges and what occurred in them.
2. Journal regarding three areas of these relationship challenges that you need to improve on and what skills you need to utilize to transform your interactions with others.

3. Journal the reason these relationships skills are key to transforming a ministry culture within the body of Christ.
4. Write an apology letter to someone you know have experienced church hurt. Use these skills to express to them how their situation should have been handled.
5. Begin implementing these applicable tools immediately in your daily interactions. Journal your experiences.

THE ART OF TRUE ACCOUNTABILITY

From Dr. Taquetta Bakers Book, "Healing The Wounded Leader"

This chapter is to help leaders discern the people who really want to change and are ready to change. And to stop leaders from wasting time with those who are not ready to change or do not want to change.

Accountability Versus Consensus
Often, we will wait until we have made a decision about a matter then present it to our leadership, spiritual parent/children, friend, spouse, God, etc., as us desiring accountability to the decision we have made. What we fail to realize is no one can make a true account for something they did not initially know about or agree to.

When I go to the bank, I have to put my money in the account FIRST before there can be an account for my money, and before the bank can be accountable for my money. If I have $500 but go to Walmart and spend $300. I cannot then go to the bank and say I am depositing $500 when I only have $200. I have already made a decision and came into agreement with Walmart about the money I spent. The bank cannot give an account or be accountable to funds I have already spent and made a decision about. They can only respect, give an opinion, or come into consensus on the decision that I chose to make. They however, are not accountable for it, and cannot give an account for it. They can only hope I remain accountable to the consensus I made with them.

This is the reason most decisions made in this manner fail. There is consensus but not true weight where both parties are responsible for the outcome. The other person has no real investment, as they did not partake in the decision making process.

Also because both parties were not initially consulted in the decision making process, the decision maker tends to feel entitled to make adjustments to the agreement at will without any accountability to what was initially consented upon. The person then avoids being accountable as they keep changing the agreement, while never really reaching their goal, or self-evaluating the reason their agreement is not achieved. Though it is never actually spoken or acknowledged, the prideful truth is there is no real accountability when one person is the main and "only" shareholder in the decision making.

Sidebar Wisdom: Both leaders and members engage in this misperception of accountability. We must recognize that is not true accountability, and thus it produces little to no results in meeting goals, maintaining standards, and maturing in the Lord.

Accountability Gives an Account

Many times a person will take a matter to their leader, spiritual parent/child, friend, spouse, and/or God, and will make accountability agreements with them, but will not want to take blame when he or she is not accountable to the vows and covenants that were made. Accountability is all about blame. It is all about giving an account for the agreement at hand.

Dictionary.com defines *accountability* as:
1. subject to the obligation to report, explain, or justify something; responsible; answerable.
2. capable of being explained; explicable; explainable.
3. synonyms are as followed: answerability, blameworthiness, liability, responsibility, burden, fault, guilt, incrimination, liability

When we enter an accountability agreement, we are obligated to:
- Report on our progress or lack thereof.
- Clearly explain the reason we have or have not progressed.
- Attempt to justify our actions without using poor excuses or divert from our irresponsibility.
- Answer questions and concerns that surface regarding our actions or lack of.
- Take responsibility and blame for the progress or lack of progress.
- Be open to constructive criticism and hearing truth about the changes and improvements needed to ensure accountability.
- Repent to God and the person as necessary.
- Examine if cycles of sabotage and destiny killing spirits are at work.
- Examine strongholds such as spirits of laziness, sluggardness, irresponsibility, disobedience, anti-submissiveness, rebellion, lawlessness, etc. Break their powers off your life and implement practices to rid yourself of anyway they have embedded their fruit in your personality and character.

- Encourage one another in each of your abilities and capabilities to fulfill the agreement.
- Re-evaluate the agreement, and be honest about whether we are capable of achieving it or not, or whether we are willing to invest the time to achieve it or not. This is important because we do not want to waste the other person's time investing in an agreement that we are not willing or ready to be accountable to.
- If we are ready, then make any necessary changes and begin again. If we are not ready, then move on and let that be that.

Accountability Requires Discipline

Often, we enter accountability agreements from the potential of the person, but not the reality of where they are in life. Though we are striving to achieve the potential, the foundation of accountability is based on that which can be clearly identified. Therefore, true accountability requires:

- Discipline
- Focus
- Maturity
- Responsibility

We have to be honest with ourselves and with people about what each party can handle regarding accountability for the maturity level each of us are at. People mean well and have a mind to change or succeed, but do not always have the heart to change or succeed. Though accountability agreements are made to grow a person into maturity regarding a matter, we must make sure the drive, desire and conviction is present to really work an accountability plan. Without these three ingredients, the parties involved may not incur the discipline, focus, maturity and responsibility needed to fulfill that agreement.

People must also understand that when you enter an accountability agreement, you are establishing covenants and oaths, and vows are being made.

> ***Deuteronomy 23:21-22*** *When thou shalt vow a vow unto the LORD thy God, thou shalt not slack to pay it: for the LORD thy God will surely require it of thee; and it would be sin in thee.*

James 5:12 But above all things, my brethren, swear not, neither by heaven, neither by the earth, neither by any other oath: but let your yea be yea; and your nay, nay; lest ye fall into condemnation.

When accountability agreements are broken, we must give an account to God for our actions so that we do not reap the consequences of an unpaid vow. This is the reason it is so important to watch what we commit to, and being slow to agree when we are not sure if we are ready to follow through on the matter at hand. It is okay to take time to examine an agreement before God and make sure you have the drive, desire and conviction to work that plan.

Accountability in Covenant Relationships
Often times, we say we are accountable to our covenant relationship, but much of what we call accountability is us getting the other person to agree, conform or accept our ideas and actions. An authentic spiritual relationship involves legitimate accountability where each party is willing and open to carry the burden of that covenant agreement, and is open to receiving truth from one another. Truth is spoken with respect and honor for one another, and sincere concern for the state of one another's soul and walk with God. If there is initial disagreement of what is being spoken, examining what has been shared before God is vital to making sure deception of the enemy is not at work.

The enemy wants to alter and kill your progress, process, covenant relationship and destiny. If God spoke it then he will confirm it. If you do not receive initial clarity, then allow what has been spoken to remain conscious within you until you are sure it is of God or not of God. This will save you from being deceived if the word was indeed true, and from any seeds that the enemy will try to sow through disagreement; as often times we agree to disagree and think that is resolution. The subject was dropped, but true accountability was not in operation.

Amos 3:3 Can two walk together, except they be agreed?

New Living Bible Can two people walk together without agreeing on the direction?

When we agree to disagree, we are actually operating in a false peace and superficial harmony, as our actions present as we are on one accord, but our spirits are divided. Also, the disagreement is lying dormant until the next time there is a challenge or search for truth.

The reason this is important is because accountability means we each take blame and ownership for our actions and because we are in covenant, we are affected by one another's actions. We each are equally responsible as if we have committed the act personally. Each of our actions must be reported one to another, justified, and explained; and through our covenant, we are contending that we answer and are responsible to one another and to God for one another. With that being said, if either of us are engaging in actions that cannot be vouched for, with no regard for the "truth" the other person has spoken, we are violating our covenant of honor one to the other and unto God. We are in consensus, but not in covenant.

It is important for the body of Christ to mature in this area. We jump from relationship to relationship and enter covenants with no regard to the spiritual ramifications. We have to learn healthy relationship skills, and study the biblical truths regarding fellowshipping and walking together, so we can grow in relationship with one another. If we contend we are journeying in life with God, then we will never bypass true accountability. It is an essential discipline necessary to maintain covenant with him and to those he puts in our lives. Do not allow unresolved relationship issues and irresponsibility to thwart your ability to be accountable. Decreeing healing and increased maturity in the things of the Lord is your portion! SHIFT!

Homework Explorations:
1. List at least four principles you learned about concerning accountability.
2. Search out your accountability partners as it relates to this chapter. Journal in detail, areas where you need to come into true accountability in your relationships.
3. Journal how you do with receiving constructive criticism. Journal what thoughts and feelings surface. Journal ways you need to improve with receiving constructive criticism.

THE VALUE OF KINGDOM COVENANT

COVENANT WITH GOD

A covenant is a pledge or allegiance between two or more parties. An agreement within a covenant breeds harmony, cooperation, compliance and a willingness to compromise or submit oneself for the good of the covenant or for the sake of the other person to which you are in covenant with. Covenants with God are rooted in his word and will for our lives. God, therefore, will not go against anything that does not align with his likeness - his nature or character - his word and his will. God, however, is always faithful to his covenant with us as his word is always true, valid and fruitful.

> ***Isaiah 55:11*** *So shall my word be that goeth forth out of my mouth: it shall not return unto me void,*
> *but it shall accomplish that which I please, and it shall prosper in the thing whereto I sent it.*

Covenants tend to be stunted and fruitless when we are out of agreement with what we have agreed upon with God, that God did not agree with, and when we are operating in another covenant that does not align with his nature, character - his word and will. It is essential to make sure that God agrees with what we are doing and that it is a part of his will for our lives. Performing consistent covenant checks will aide in making sure agreement is in order. Also, making sure you have the peace and word of God before proceeding in an area that may be suspect is also effective in keeping covenant with God. Confusion, uneasiness, questioning that causes turmoil or ungodly fear and frustration can be indicators that you have stepped outside of covenant or that you do not have God's blessing regarding something you are doing.

> ***Proverbs 10:22*** *The blessing of the Lord, it maketh rich, and he addeth no sorrow with it.*

<u>Sorrow</u> is *eseb* in Hebrew and means:
1. an earthen vessel; usually (painful) toil; also a pang (whether of body or mind)
2. grievous, idol, labor, sorrow
3. pain, hurt, toil, hardship, pain, hurt, offense

Agreement breeds peace. If you do not have peace then you may be experiencing sorrow that comes with a breath of covenant.

GODLY COVENANT RELATIONSHIPS

Godly covenants are not designed by how you want them to be, but by how God desires them to be. That means when God releases a covenant relationship to you, he has a purpose for that relationship. It often has a personal and ministerial purpose that is meant to represent him, glorify him, advance you and that person so that you and that person can advance the kingdom.

Godly covenants possess the character and nature of God, his principles, his standards, his laws, his fruit and his spirit. It is meant to further establish you in the fullness of salvation as it relates to our fellowship and family institution with one another. The negative things that occur in natural family relationships was never God's design. So with the reestablishment of covenant through the cross comes the redemption of pure covenant relationships.

That person may feel like your natural family — Like you have known them all your life. However, they are not your natural family. They are your spiritual family. Therefore, your interactions with them are from a spiritual perspective, and encompasses a godly foundation and a godly establishment of healthy covenant.

- ❖ That means you cannot talk to them any kind of way.
- ❖ You cannot treat them any kind of way.
- ❖ You cannot take them for granted.
- ❖ You cannot make them pay for whatever hurts you have from your natural family or other relationships, as they are your spiritual family not your natural family.

The relationship covenant in and of itself will expose and come for anything that is not like God. It is designed to expose, reject and eject anything that is not like God. That is because it is not meant to have sin, transgressions, unhealthiness, soul wounds, heart issues and ungodly characteristics. These matters are exposed so deliverance and healing can occur to bring you, that person and the relationship into the pure wellness of salvation.

Covenant relationships have godly order:

- **Husband and Wife - The Husband Is The Head**

    Ephesians 6:22-29 Wives, submit yourselves unto your own husbands, as unto the Lord. For the husband is the head of the wife, even as Christ is the head of the church: and he is the saviour of the body. Therefore as the church is subject unto Christ, so let the wives be to their own husbands in everything. Husbands, love your wives, even as Christ also loved the church, and gave himself for it; That he might sanctify and cleanse it with the washing of water by the word, That he might present it to himself a glorious church, not having spot, or wrinkle, or any such thing; but that it should be holy and without blemish. So ought men to love their wives as their own bodies. He that loveth his wife loveth himself. For no man ever yet hated his own flesh; but nourisheth and cherisheth it, even as the Lord the church.

    1Corinthians 11:3 But I would have you know, that the head of every man is Christ; and the head of the woman [is] the man; and the head of Christ [is] God.

- **Spiritual Parenting, Mentoring, Or Leadership**

    In this type of relationship, the spiritual parent, mentor and leader is the head. Whether for a season or lifetime, they are required to govern the life and soul of that spiritual child, mentee, or sheep. If you are trying to dictate to the parent, mentor and leader how they should lead you then you are out of order. God gives them the blueprint and will give it to you as well, but they are the head of it and see farther than you do regarding it. It is important to make sure God called you as a child, mentee or sheep to this type of relationship because if he did, then you have to submit and trust this person with your life and soul. Without submission and trust, the covenant relationship will lack fullness and consistency, and will be stifled, frustrated, and even breached.

    Often our focus is trying to trust the person so we can submit, but the greatest question and focus is do you trust God; and are you willing to submit to who God is putting in and over your life. If you focus on trusting God and his purpose for the relationship, it will make trusting the covenant overseer easier.

Covenants will expose your rebellion and disobedience because it requires submission and trust. If you have difficulty submitting and trusting, you will manifest rebellion and disobedience. Most likely what you are revealing through that relationship is a manifestation of rebellion and disobedience in your covenant with God.

Spiritual parenting is intended to be a lifelong covenant relationship. Spiritual children possess the spiritual DNA of their spiritual parents and are imparted and carry some facet of the spiritual parent's legacy and mantle into the next generation. The relationship is very personal as the spiritual parent is responsible for birthing the child's destiny via prayer and intercession, and helping to prune their character and life, so they can sustain in their destiny and calling; along with the child being groomed as successors of the spiritual parent's mantle and legacy. These relationships occur a lot in fivefold ministries. However, it is important to note that just because a person is your apostle, leader, etc., that does not automatically make them your spiritual parent. Also I do want to note that an apostle, leader, or mentor can help birth and groom you in fashions of your destiny and calling without being your spiritual parent. Allow God to define your relationship and if you desire a spiritual parent, seek him as to who that is to be, and wait on him to release them into your life.

> ***1Timothy 1:18-20 The Message Bible*** *I'm passing this work on to you, my son Timothy. The prophetic word that was directed to you prepared us for this. All those prayers are coming together now so you will do this well, fearless in your struggle, keeping a firm grip on your faith and on yourself. After all, this is a fight we're in. There are some, you know, who by relaxing their grip and thinking anything goes have made a thorough mess of their faith. Hymenaeus and Alexander are two of them. I let them wander off to Satan to be taught a lesson or two about not blaspheming.*
>
> ***Isaiah 61:9*** *Then their offspring will be known among the nations, And their descendants in the midst of the peoples. All who see them will recognize them Because they are the offspring whom the LORD has blessed.*

> ***Psalms 127:3-5*** *Behold, children are a gift of the LORD, The fruit of the womb is a reward. Like arrows in the hand of a warrior, So are the children of one's youth. How blessed is the man whose quiver is full of them; They will not be ashamed When they speak with their enemies in the gate.*
>
> ***Galatians 4:19*** *My little children, of whom I travail in birth (labor in pain) again until Christ be formed in you.*

Mentoring tends to be a seasonal covenant relationship. This can be different seasons throughout your life with the same or even different mentors. This type of relationship may encompass impartation and training for a specific purpose to bring deliverance, healing, awakening and cultivation of an intricate area of destiny. Relationship can be personal so that deliverance, healing, awakening and cultivation can take place. Relationship can also be surface if mentoring is done through a class, network that is not hands on, book study, association such as online following, seasonally visiting a ministry, yet deliverance and healing, etc., is still able to manifest. Mentors can birth specific areas of destiny in a person if God requires and the person will receive impartation from the mentor's mantle and calling, but there is often no DNA components, generational purpose, or successorship attached to the relationship.

> ***Ephesians 4:11-16*** *And he gave some, apostles; and some, prophets; and some, evangelists; and some, pastors and teachers; For the perfecting of the saints, for the work of the ministry, for the edifying of the body of Christ: Till we all come in the unity of the faith, and of the knowledge of the Son of God, unto a perfect man, unto the measure of the stature of the fulness of Christ: That we henceforth be no more children, tossed to and fro, and carried about with every wind of doctrine, by the sleight of men, and cunning craftiness, whereby they lie in wait to deceive; But speaking the truth in love, may grow up into him in all things, which is the head, even Christ: From whom the whole body fitly joined together and compacted by that which every joint supplieth, according to the effectual working in the measure of every part, maketh increase of the body unto the edifying of itself in love*

Leadership can include instructors, pastors, and leaders of groups you are a part of, and can be for a moment in time, season and sometimes a lifetime. Training, equipping, and shepherding is done to enlighten, empower, advance, or cover one's spiritual walk. Relationship can be surface, impersonal, and more about instruction, protecting salvation, teaching and equipping rather than personal relationship.

> *1Corinthians 4:15-17* *For though ye have ten thousand instructors in Christ, yet have ye not many fathers: for in Christ Jesus I have begotten you through the gospel. Wherefore I beseech you, be ye followers of me. For this cause have I sent unto you Timotheus, who is my beloved son, and faithful in the Lord, who shall bring you into remembrance of my ways which be in Christ, as I teach every where in every church.*

<u>Begotten</u> is <u>*gennao*̄ in Greek and means:</u>
1. to procreate (properly, of the father, but by extension of the mother)
2. figuratively, to regenerate: — bear, beget, be born, bring forth, conceive
3. be delivered of, gender, make, spring

Spiritual mothers and fathers birth you. Mentors and leaders instruct and impart into you.

- **<u>Peer Covenants (Friendships, Sisterships, Brotherly Relationships)</u>**
  Peers are heads of one another - mutually accountable to one another. Though there are instances where one may lead the other. This is because there are times where one is stronger than the other or may need the other.

  > *Ecclesiastes 4:9-12* *Two are better than one, because they have a good [more satisfying] reward for their labor; For if they fall, the one will lift up his fellow. But woe to him who is alone when he falls and has not another to lift him up! Again, if two lie down together, then they have warmth; but how can one be warm alone? And though a man might prevail against him who is alone, two will withstand him. A threefold cord is not quickly broken.*

Basically in this type of covenant, you are both submitting to one another so you both can grow personally and together.

> ***Proverbs 27:17*** *Iron sharpeneth iron; so a man sharpeneth the countenance of his friend.*
>
> ***The Message Bible*** *You use steel to sharpen steel, and one friend sharpens another.*

Iron is sharpened by rubbing it against another piece of sharp iron. When two pieces of iron, especially iron blades rub together, both become sharper. Also, an equipping is occurring as both are empowering the other through the connection they have with one another. Both begin to change and transform while becoming more refined. Each are then more efficient for use.

Sharp means "*to become keen, acute, alert, watchful, defined, cutting edge, swift, tapered, fierce.*"

When covenants do not sharpen one another, the relationship becomes dull, slow, lazy, un-useful and blurred in vision. Feelings are easily hurt due to unspoken and unmet expectations flaring. These expectations tend to out way the level of iron production manifesting in the relationship. If the relationship is unfruitful, stagnant, or not beneficial, check the iron production. For whatever reason, either you or the other person is not investing in the relationship. Someone has to start sharpening the other for production to manifest. If you are waiting on the other person, then you are already demonstrating that you have some issues with investing in relationships or in that person.

Examine yourself and that covenant relationship; explore if God is releasing you from the relationship if there is no sharpening productivity or seek him for what you need to do to activate sharpening productivity if he desires you to remain in the covenant relationship.

AGREEMENT REGARDING COVENANT

> ***Amos 3:3*** *Can two walk together, except they be agreed?*

New Living Bible *Can two people walk together without agreeing on the direction?*

There has to be agreement regarding the direction of the covenant relationship which is the reason praying and seeking God for the purpose is important. Once you agree upon the purpose, there has to be agreement in how he says it is to be walked out. Sometimes you may not like how God desires to unfold the covenant relationship. At times, his way may make you feel vulnerable, exposed, cut, pruned, challenged, chastised and punked, etc., but it all has greater purpose of healing and governing your soul and shaping your life and character for sustaining destiny. The more you become like him, the less you feel or have these perspectives. Your flesh and emotions become subjected to your spirit, where your spirit embodies submission, honor, and obedience to loving and living for God in such admiration, that your will in life is to do what the father does and be all he wants you to be.

> *John 4:34* *Jesus saith unto them, My meat is to do the will of him that sent me, and to finish his work.*

You become self-sacrificing in eating whatever food God gives you, however he chooses to give it to you, to please him.

> *Psalms 40:8* *I delight to do Your will, O my God; Your law is within my heart."*

> *John 5:30* *I can do nothing by Myself; I judge only as I hear. And My judgment is just, because I do not seek My own will, but the will of Him who sent Me.*

> *John 6:38* *For I have come down from heaven, not to do My own will, but to do the will of Him who sent Me.*

> *John 8:29* *He who sent Me is with Me. He has not left Me alone, because I always do what pleases Him."*

> *John 17:4* *I have glorified You on earth by accomplishing the work You gave Me to do.*

COVENANT ACCOUNTABILITY

Accountability in true covenant is not trying to get the other person to agree, conform or accept your ideas and actions, especially if they are not aligned with God or are not what God is requiring at that season of your life. Accountability is knowing what the will and purpose of God is and submitting to one another in agreement to what he is speaking. If there is a head to the relationship such as in marriage, spiritual parenting, mentoring, etc., that person guides and governs the purpose of the covenant, as God is holding them accountable for bringing his will to pass. You as the wife, spiritual child, mentee, are accountable to them and you follow them as they follow God. You however, do not get to change God's plan because you do not want to be accountable or have problems with submission, trust and obedience, or you have soul issues that cause you to be challenged by the covenant principles and standards.

Refusing to be accountable can cause a delay, stifling, abortion and even breaching of covenant. So many people are living in God's permissive will rather than true purpose - his perfected will - because they refuse godly accountability. God's permissive will is what you allow him to do regarding your destiny. His perfect will is what he has ordained for you regarding destiny. Many live in his permissive will and think it is his perfect will because he is not rebutting or punishing them for their actions. They feel no conviction or he is not convicting them for their actions. It feels good and is comfortable so it must be God, it produces blessings so it must be him.

God's permissive will only produces a measure of destiny. There is often a slow or minimal progression of destiny. Often, you cycle without ever receiving and reaching the fullness of the prophecies and promises of God for your life.

God's perfect will empowers you to go from level to level - glory to glory in him. You are constantly and consistently producing, reproducing, multiplying and journeying in dominion with him.

> ***Genesis 1:28*** *And God blessed them, and God said unto them, Be fruitful, and multiply, and replenish the earth, and subdue it: and have dominion over the fish of the sea, and over the fowl of the air, and over every living thing that moveth upon the earth.*

There is a constant progression of life success, and unfolding and evolving in destiny. You clearly see God's continual hand upon your life and are always progressing in the ways, deeds, fruits, blessings and advancements of the Lord.

Check to see what your life is demonstrating. The fruit of your life will not lie to you. It is speaking clearly as to whether you are living in his permissive will or his perfect will. SHIFT!

> *Matthew 7:16* By their fruit you will recognize them. Do people pick grapes from thornbushes, or figs from thistles?
>
> *John 7:17* If anyone's will is to do God's will, he will know whether the teaching is from God or whether I am speaking on my own authority.
>
> *Psalms 37:23* The steps of a man are established by the Lord, when he delights in his way.
>
> *Psalms 27:11* Teach me your way, O Lord, and lead me on a level path because of my enemies.
>
> *2Corinthians 3:18* And all of us, as with unveiled face, [because we] continued to behold [in the Word of God] as in a mirror the glory of the Lord, are constantly being transfigured into His very own image in ever increasing splendor and from one degree of glory to another; [for this comes] from the Lord [Who is] the Spirit.

I do want to state that when I use the word order, submission and obedience that I am not talking about being controlled, abused, mishandled, or having no say. Many cringe when the words order, submission and obedience are used in godly relationship yet, they do all of these things every day on a job or when they are striving to get their desires or needs met. They surrender themselves and order themselves with whatever is necessary to get what they want, even at the expense of selling their progress, soul, and/or selling themselves short.

The person God ordains for you in covenant relationship should have God's heart for you and their heart is demonstrated in how they care for and guide you. Even if they have to correct, rebuke, and speak blatant truth to you, put boundaries in place, reassess boundaries, etc., God's heart will be demonstrated. Your flesh and heart may not like it but your spirit knows they have the heart of God for you. This is often what keeps drawing you to them even though you may be challenged to submit fully to the covenant.

I also want to state that many can assume that correction and not getting their way is being controlled, abused or mishandled which is the biggest fear challenges with surrendering in covenant relationship. But the word talks about the chastening the God.

> ***Hebrews 12:7-8** 7 If ye endure chastening, God dealeth with you as with sons; for what son is he whom the father chasteneth not? 8 But if ye be without chastisement, whereof all are partakers, then are ye bastards, and not sons.*

<u>Chastening is *paideia* in Greek and means:</u>
1. tutorage, i.e. education or training; by implication, disciplinary correction: — chastening, chastisement, instruction, nurture
2. the whole training and education of children (which relates to the cultivation of mind and morals, and employs for this purpose now commands and admonitions, now reproof and punishment)
3. It also includes the training and care of the body, whatever in adults also cultivates the soul, esp. by correcting mistakes and curbing passions
4. instruction which aims at increasing virtue chastisement
5. chastening, (of the evils with which God visits men for their amendment

Chastening is not just about correcting. It is about instructing, training, educating, nurturing, caring, restoring, enlightening, cultivating, empowering, and bringing discipline and sustaining consistency in your sonship with the Lord. Your covenant will chasten you through the heart of God for you. It will not be because they want to Lord over you, but because they want what God is showing them for you.

God is adamant about fivefold ministry being in operation in this hour. He is mandating team work and covenants to produce his kingdom in the earth.

In order to engage covenant you have to:

- ❖ Be willing to give up your vulnerabilities and fears regarding being hurt and embrace covenant.
- ❖ Journey in the SHIFTS that covenant takes, as just when you think you are settled in covenant, God may unveil something new about you, that person, himself, and/or the purpose of the covenant. Your heart, mind and emotions will have to be subjected to the spirit work of covenant that God is doing. The more resistant you are in this area, the more drama you endure in your covenant relationships.
- ❖ Get healed of broken family dynamics and past relationship hurts. Recognize triggers of old hurts and deal with them as they surface. Do not let them linger where you are casting old hurts on your new covenant relationships. Do not make covenant pay for what others did.
- ❖ Be delivered from rejection, the orphan spirit and the vagabond spirit - these spirits cause you to view your covenants as threats and with a critical proving eye rather than as safety nets. You are always waiting on them to fail you so you can prove the covenant was not a God send, prove why you do not trust people, and prove why you should be a long ranger. It is difficult to embrace, settle, and trust when you need deliverance in these areas. You sabotage love, togetherness, and tend to provoke drama that kill covenant relationships as these spirits will not allow you to rest in the love, unity and bond of covenant relationship.
- ❖ Receive vision from God about who you covenant with personally, ministerially, and in business. Ask for revelation of their purpose in your life, your purpose in their life, and be committed to sacrificing yourself in the covenant to receive what God is saying for the covenant.
- ❖ Learn and utilize healthy communication, conflict resolution and coping skills. Covenants protect and care for one another's hearts. You should care about how you hurt and treat your covenants.
- ❖ Be open to asking the hard questions, confronting in love and honor but in truth.
- ❖ Apologizing and forgiving quickly, while recognizing that conflict and differences does not mean the covenant is breached. Conflict and differences are used to get you and the covenant in alignment with the agreement, will and purpose of God. That is the reason the word says "how can we walk together except we agree." There

is a work of agreement that will have to be done in covenant. It takes conscious work to build healthy covenant. God uses those close to us as safety places to prune character, his nature, his fruit, and identity into us, so we can align in covenant with him and one another. The more you embrace covenant, the more the heart of God should be embedded in you for covenant and souls in general.

- ❖ Covenant can be breached through betrayal and will require reconciliation and restoration to establish renewed covenant. This takes a lot of work but can be done. You will not return to who you were to one another as that obviously could not sustain the relationship. It takes a conscious work to restore to a new place, as betrayal changes each person and the dynamics of the relationship. Betrayal causes the old covenant to die and a new covenant to surface. It will be important to seek God about what the new covenant is and looks like and reconcile and restore from that new posture.
- ❖ Your covenants should build you up and even draw you into unity and love with your other covenant relationships. If your covenants are feeding your hurts, pains, fears, are full of gossip, envy, being degrading of others, are separating you from covenants that you know God has for you, then you need to check if this is a true covenant relationship or if the person or people you are in covenant with is operating in the character or nature of God. As your covenant should never be built on disunity with others but in unity with God and his wellness and healthiness for your life.

Ephesians 4:1-3 The Amplified Bible *I THEREFORE, the prisoner for the Lord, appeal to and beg you to walk (lead a life) worthy of the [divine] calling to which you have been called [with behavior that is a credit to the summons to God's service, Living as becomes you] with complete lowliness of mind (humility) and meekness (unselfishness, gentleness, mildness), with patience, bearing with one another and making allowances because you love one another. Be eager and strive earnestly to guard and keep the harmony and oneness of [and produced by] the Spirit in the binding power of peace.*

<u>Peace in this scripture is *eirēne* and means:</u>
1. to join); peace (literally or figuratively); by implication, prosperity
2. one, peace, quietness, rest, + set at one again
3. a state of national tranquility, exemption from the rage and havoc of war,

4. peace between individuals, i.e. harmony, concord security, safety, prosperity, felicity, (because peace and harmony make and keep things safe and prosperous) of the Messiah's peace, the way that leads to peace (salvation) of Christianity, the tranquil state of a soul assured of its salvation through Christ, and so fearing nothing from God and content with its earthly lot

Meditate on that passage of scripture and on the definition of peace and check your covenants before God. Fix anything that is hindering God's true peace. Separate from relationships that do not possess God's true peace.

> ***New Living Bible*** *Therefore I, a prisoner for serving the Lord, beg you to lead a life worthy of your calling, for you have been called by God. Always be humble and gentle. Be patient with each other, making allowance for each other's faults because of your love. Make every effort to keep yourselves united in the Spirit, binding yourselves together with peace.*

Homework Explorations:
1. What are your thoughts about covenant relationships now that you have read this chapter?
2. Journal areas where you need to improve your covenant relationship with God.
3. Journal areas where you need to improve your covenant relationships with spiritual parents, mentors, and leaders.

TRAINING & EQUIPPING

This chapter will provide suggestions for how to train and equip your team and members in general. Training and equipping in fivefold ministry is constant and ongoing as it is a significant part of fivefold ministry. The members need to be trained in whatever the ministry vision is, and in their destinies and callings. Training is not limited to ministry as fivefold ministry is about equipping members in lifestyle living with God and for the advancement of the vision. Therefore, training and equipping can be for:

- Educational Purposes (e.g. Day Care Centers, Head Start Programs, Grades 1st - 12th, G.E.D. Programs, College Courses)
- Business Classes
- Employment Assistance Trainings
- Leadership Development
- Professional Trades & Certifications
- Licensing & Ordination In Ministry & Fivefold Offices
- Ministry Training To Evangelize & Minister To Souls
- Spiritual Warfare, Spiritual Mapping, & Training On Enemy Tactics
- The World's System, Idolatry Occult & Witchcraft Systems
- Revival Reformation
- New Members Classes, Ongoing Discipleship To Build People
- Strategic Workshops & Trainings Related To The Advancement Of The Vision
- Vision Casting
- Healthy Marriage, Family & Generational Evolvement & Interaction
- Teaching applicable life skills, such as conflict and communication skills, anger management, social skills, interpersonal relationship skills, character building, unity and healthy fellowship, financing and investment
- Destiny Attainment & Life Fulfillment
- Community Courses For Neighborhood & Regional Development (The community should be able to come and be developed personally and spiritually)
- Counseling, Mentoring, Coaching Training & Centers
- Housing & Real Estate (Owning land is key to owning the region; teaching and equipping property investment, owning land,

building kingdom businesses and organizations is important for revival reformation)
- Laws & Politics & Operating In Political Arenas (This is very important as laws continue to become more anti-Christ. The Body of Christ needs to be abreast of the laws, how to change and impact laws, and their rights as Christians).

Have Trainings Instead of Traditional Services

Trainings can even be done on Sundays as fivefold ministry does not operate by traditional church patterns, so it is ok to train instead of having regular church services. My ministry does not have traditional Sunday services or programs. We have services, trainings, etc., as God leads us and according to the need and pattern of our vision. This has helped to advance the growth and acceleration of our team and the vision. This is more beneficial than trying to figure out what to preach that is more out of traditional obligation than what is really in line with the vision and personal and spiritual development. These trainings are just as fulfilling as services and we have experienced deliverance, healings, transformation and miracles as if we were in a service.

Hands on Training

As my team and members learn, they are provided opportunities to activate what they learn. They are given assignments within the ministry, community, online, at services and events. They are allowed to pray, teach, preach, prophecy, train, equip and impart. They may be given prayer and prophetic assignments ahead of time so they can seek the Lord on what he desires them to pray for and prophecy. And sometimes its spontaneous praying and prophecy. I have them turn in sermons and teachings a few days before an event then I give them feedback. They implement the feedback and then submit it again for further direction. They then go forth in their perspective assignment and I provide feedback after they finish teaching, preaching, training etc. When we do have ongoing services, my vision carriers and main leaders are placed on a ministry rotation schedule. They assist with ministering at the services and I, the main vision carrier, only do all of the ministering as the Lord leads. Otherwise, we work the schedule so each vision carrier is given the opportunity to train and grow in their ministry gifts and calling. It also helps members receive from all the vision carriers and they are not just expecting impartation from me.

Depending on their gifts and callings, vision carriers and members may be given assignments to pursue in the community. For example, ministering at shelters, prisons, nursing homes, schools, colleges, volunteering, evangelizing at different locations and events, partnering with other ministries for community events, attending community and political meetings, creating programs and events. They are trained and equipped in how to minister in these different arenas and so they are equipped when they are sent out. The assignments also help to further equip them as well as assist with us reaching the lost, unhealed and being a spiritual advocate for God in the community.

Sometimes they are sent to attend training seminars in business, economic development, and any other areas that benefit their destiny and calling. As some trainings I may not be able to supply but they are occurring within the community, online or abroad. It is okay if members attend such professional trainings. The more equipped they are, the better they are able to impart what they learn into the members of the ministry. I do suggest members ask the vision carriers if ministries, businesses, and organizations that they desire to gleam from are appropriate before attending events or listening to sermons and teachings. People are releasing all kinds of ideologies that are not of God, rooted in God, or is in effort to sway people from God. I suggest making this a requirement as there is safety in a multitude of counseling.

> ***Proverbs 11:14*** *Where no counsel is, the people fall: but in the multitude of counsellors there is safety.*

I strive to use all the gifts that are available in the ministry so we will make room for the artist, poets, exhorters and dance ministers at our services, meetings and events. They are encouraged to use their gifts and to view it as a daily part of life and how God wants to speak and minister. We even encourage and activate children by allowing them to be used in their perspective gifts within services and events. They may be a part of the praise team, dance ministry, asked to draw, write a poem, prophecy, pray, etc. The more children are trained in the ways of God, the more they will enjoy it and it will become a part of their identity and destiny development.

Learn and activate should be the motto of fivefold ministry. No one should be sitting on the pew. Everyone has some gift or calling they should be doing for the body of Christ. It is important to get people motivated to do daily destiny with God.

Ministry Tracks & Mentoring

In my ministry, each member receives a monthly mentoring session with me or one of the vision carriers and they work a ministry track. The mentoring sessions aide to personally journey with them in their destiny and calling. They receive prayer, deliverance, healing, direction, strategy and feedback on personal and ministry areas they need to work on and have progressed in. They are built up in their destiny and calling and given direction and homework assignments to improve their lives, family, and relationship with God and destiny.

The track created for them can be related to licensing or ordination, their destiny or calling, or areas of discipleship where they need to grow in their character, building a relationship with God, increasing faith, understanding of the gospel, dealing with sin and deliverance issues, studying of the Bible, prayer and fasting, life disciplines, breaking of generational curses and cycles. The tracks can be changed as God leads to ensure they are working on what he desires as the tracks are tailored to the needs of the member for personal development. It may include prayer assignments, homework assignments, reading materials such as books and topics to study, google searches to obtain information and study, sermons and teachings to listen to. I have placed many teachings and trainings from trusted individuals into a Dropbox folder that my mentors and I are able to access and give to members to study on particular topics. I highly suggest a feature of this nature because then the members are acquiring information that you trust and that you know is in line with the vision.

I write curriculum and so members are able to access my books and use them as study tools. My overseer has written over a hundred books so we utilize her resources as study materials that are added to the tracks. I recommend making your sermons, teachings, and training information available for further study and adding them as study tools on the tracks of present and future members. The tracks may include assignments in the community related to their destiny and calling. It may entail pursuing training outside the ministry at a trusted location for further personal and/or ministry development.

As members have tracks to work, they always have something to work on daily. They are not dependent on a service or event to build them up. They are learning how to be daily learners with God. They are learning how to be disciplined where destiny and personal development is a lifestyle...

Example Of Tracks:

Consistency Track:
- Google articles on consistency and journal what you learned. Turn in assignment by January 22, 2019.
- Seek God for strongholds that hinder your consistency. Obtain five scriptures to combat these strongholds. Pray against them daily from now until your next mentoring session. Journal your experiences and progress.
- Practice daily what you learned on consistency.
- Read the book: Self Discipline: 10 Day Self Discipline Blueprint by Callum Rowling. Write a paper on what you learned by February 22nd, 2019.
- Pray for 30 minutes at the same time every day from now until your next session. Journal your progress.

Ministry Track:

- Write a three page paper on your call to ministry. Discuss your purpose, metron, sphere, gifts, callings, etc. (August 2019)
- Attend ministry classes and workshops within the ministry that will be occurring quarterly for the next year. Complete all assignments related to those classes and workshops.
- Once a month, video yourself ministering a twenty minute message and email it to me.
- Read the following books and write a three page paper on what you learned and how it relates to your calling and destiny. Complete any homework assignments at the end of each chapter.
  1. Prayers That Shift Atmospheres Taquetta Baker (September 2019)
  2. Awakening Regional Revival Taquetta Baker (October 2019)
  3. Discerning The Voice of God Taquetta Baker (November 2019)
  4. The Gifted Church Jackie Green (January 2020)
  5. Deliverance 101 Jackie Green (February 2020)

6. Living In The Kingdom 101 Jackie Green (March 2020)
7. Living In The Kingdom 102 Jackie Green (April 2020)
8. Leadership 101 Jackie Green (May 2020) 16. Leadership 102 Jackie Green (April 2021)
9. Christ Jesus 101 Jackie Green (June 2020) 18. Christ Jesus 102 Jackie Green (June 2021)
10. Book of Acts Jackie Green (July 2020)

Other Ways To Train & Equip

- Workshops
- Conferences
- Mentoring & Coaching
- Online Equipping- by attending trainings & conferences at other ministries, businesses, etc.
- Ongoing Online & Community Ministry Groups – e.g. you can have a fivefold ministry group for all members. This is a great way to fellowship daily and train on respective topics. You can have groups tailored to specific issues, skills, destinies and callings and train and dialog in those groups.
- Online & Ministry Network Groups – These are groups with like individuals across the body of Christ or in relations to professions or interest.
- Online Zoom Teachings & Webinars - These are some ways to train and equip via internet with large groups of people.

APOSTOLIC PROTOCOL

As members mature into releasing their own visions, they should meet with the main vision carrier to discuss what they believe God has granted to their hands. Sometimes, their vision can be submitted under the structure of the main vision and the government of the main vision carrier. This postures their vision to grow with and within the main fivefold vision; it also helps to expand the main vision and the body of Christ as a whole. All members must know protocol regarding procedures to releasing their visions so what they are releasing, teaching, and establishing can have covering, accountability and kingdom government. And so that it can be integral, successful and impactful to the people it is to reach and to regional revival reformation. I suggest making apostolic protocol a part of your new members class and policy and procedure booklet so members are clear on the procedure to releasing a vision and so that they know it is welcomed as a part of the main ministry vision.

Dictionary.com defines *protocol* as:
1. the customs and regulations dealing with diplomatic formality, precedence, and etiquette
2. an original draft, minute, or record from which a document, especially a treaty, is prepared
3. a supplementary international agreement
4. an agreement between states
5. an annex to a treaty giving data relating to it

Protocol is important so that the body - members and main fivefold vision functions and grows together in an effective godly manner.

> ***Ephesians 4:17*** *From whom the whole body fitly joined together and compacted by that which every joint supplieth, according to the effectual working in the measure of every part, maketh increase of the body unto the edifying of itself in love.*

Though fivefold ministry does not have religious doctrine or order, it does have sound doctrine and divine order. Sometimes when we hear the word "*order*" we shun it and we shun apostles. Order is not control or dictatorship. Even as God placed apostles first in rank regarding fivefold ministry, this was not so they could control or lord over members and the vision.

> *1Corinthians 12:28 And God hath set some in the church, first apostles, secondarily prophets, thirdly teachers, after that miracles, then gifts of healings, helps, governments, diversities of tongues.*

First is <u>*proton*</u> in Greek and means:
1. firstly (in time, place, order, or importance)
2. before, at the beginning, chiefly first
3. in any succession of things or persons
4. first in rank, influence, chief, honor, principal

Apostles are first because their office establishes foundation. Without solid foundation, the people and the vision cannot stand.

> *Matthew 7:24-27 Therefore whosoever heareth these sayings of mine, and doeth them, I will liken him unto a wise man, which built his house upon a rock: And the rain descended, and the floods came, and the winds blew, and beat upon that house; and it fell not: for it was founded upon a rock. And every one that heareth these sayings of mine, and doeth them not, shall be likened unto a foolish man, which built his house upon the sand: And the rain descended, and the floods came, and the winds blew, and beat upon that house; and it fell: and great was the fall of it.*

> *1Corinthians 3:3-15 For ye are yet carnal: for whereas there is among you envying, and strife, and divisions, are ye not carnal, and walk as men? For while one saith, I am of Paul; and another, I am of Apollos; are ye not carnal? Who then is Paul, and who is Apollos, but ministers by whom ye believed, even as the Lord gave to every man? I have planted, Apollos watered; but God gave the increase. So then neither is he that planteth any thing, neither he that watereth; but God that giveth the increase. Now he that planteth and he that watereth are one: and every man shall receive his own reward according to his own labour. For we are labourers together with God: ye are God's husbandry, ye are God's building. According to the grace of God which is given unto me, as a wise masterbuilder, I have laid the foundation, and another buildeth thereon. But let every man take heed how he buildeth thereupon. For other foundation can no man lay than that is laid, which is Jesus Christ. Now if any man build upon this foundation gold, silver, precious stones, wood, hay, stubble; Every man's work shall be made manifest: for the day shall declare it, because it shall be revealed by fire; and the fire shall try every man's work of what sort it is. If any man's work abide which he hath built thereupon, he shall receive a reward. If any man's work shall be burned, he shall suffer loss: but he himself shall be saved; yet so as by fire.*

Also, there is always a leader or a main vision carrier in every kingdom, government or arena. Someone has to take responsibility in guiding, shouldering and leading the vision and overseeing others in bringing it to pass. God has innately placed this in apostles to be the main vision carriers and to share this load with the other fivefold officers, team members, and the body of Christ as a whole. Just because some apostles misuse this authority, we cannot do away with all apostles and act like this is not God's word or design. We need apostles to be who God created them to be so we can effectively establish and build our fivefold mandates in the earth.

Apostles help bring administrative and governmental foundation and order to people, churches, ministries, businesses, organizations, specific works, people, communities, regions and nations. Order diminishes and extinguishes chaos, disorganization, cycling, stifling, and misalignment with God and the things of God. Order provides a process where we are able to uproot things in us and in the foundation of the ground to which we plant the vision that are not of God and that will be detrimental to what we are building (Study the parable of the seed in *Matthew 13* and *Luke 8*).

> *Ephesians 2:19-21 Now therefore ye are no more strangers and foreigners, but fellow citizens with the saints, and of the household of God; And are built upon the foundation of the apostles and prophets, Jesus Christ himself being the chief corner stone; In whom all the building fitly framed together groweth unto an holy temple in the Lord: In whom ye also are builded together for an habitation of God through the Spirit.*

Apostles are not designed or called to dictate to people, boss people around, takeover their position or platform, or control their destiny or vision. Apostles are gifted with the ability to receive a vision plan and strategy from God on how people, churches, ministries, businesses, organizations, specific works, communities, regions and nations operate. They also organize, teach, equip, administrate, and oversee others in working that plan and vision, such that they successfully progress in establishing God's will in the earth.

Apostolic Order Produces:
- The character and nature of God
- The will, plan, kingdom, glory and favor of God
- Power, comfort & instruction of the Holy Spirit

- Alignment/Set order/Straighten the crooked & false
- Balance
- Exposure
- Truth
- Judgment of the unhealthy & the demonic
- Deliverance
- Healing
- Breakthrough
- Freedom
- Healthiness & wellness
- Proper government & rulership
- Establishes the kingdom of God
- Liberty in the Holy Spirit
- Open heavens
- Kingdom empowerment
- Subduing of destiny
- Dominion
- Productivity
- Reproduction
- Consistency
- Sustaining success
- Clear vision to further progress successfully

If you want the will of God in your life, ministry, business, and region, then embrace and deem order a blessing and necessity to your kingdom walk. It is as well important to embrace apostles, and to recognize that God has given them the humility to establish order without abusing you or the authority that is on their lives.

> ***Titus 1:5*** *For this cause left I thee in Crete, that thou shouldest set in order the things that are wanting, and ordain elders in every city, as I had appointed thee:*
>
> ***The Amplified*** *Bible For this reason I left you [behind] in Crete, that you might set right what was defective and finish what was left undone, and that you might appoint elders and set them over the churches (assemblies) in every city as I directed you.*

Protocol breeds decency and order to the expansion of everyone's destinies, the fullness of the fivefold vision, and to the kingdom of God.

1Corinthians 14:40 Let all things be done decently and in order.

When a member does not inform the main vision carrier of visions they are releasing, they risk releasing something that works in opposition to the body of Christ, to God's word, to sound doctrine, and even to the laws of the land. The main vision carrier is not able to vouch for the revelation and doctrine they are teaching. This can cause for chaos, law suits, abortion or murder of the vision, and wounds and leading astray of sheep. To think that you do not need someone to keep you accountable to making sure your life and ministry aligns with the character and biblical principles of God is pride. Pride always leads to a major destructive fall (***Proverbs 16:18***).

Suggestive Protocols To Releasing A Vision
When members desire to release a vision (e.g. ministry, business, organization, group, school, event, etc.), they should schedule a meeting with the main vision carrier to discuss what they believe God is saying.

It would be efficient to already know the purpose, mandate, metron, and scripture foundation, of the vision. Members can learn how to write a vision plan by reading Dr. Taquetta Baker's book, "*Sustaining The Vision.*"

The meeting should:
- ✓ Examine the vision.
- ✓ Provide further insight regarding the vision and determine the timing to release the vision. This may or may not be the timing. It is important to know timing as exposing the vision too soon or when the member is not equipped to launch a vision could abort, stifle, cause hardship or warfare to them and the vision. When the vision is not sown in proper time the wrong season, or even in good ground, the enemy will steal the seeds and the fruit of the vision and cause death to it. The ground can also be unstable causing foundational issues, cracks, and even a tumbling of the vision.
- ✓ Determine whether the member is ready to release the vision; provide guidance, set timely measurable goals regarding the personal preparations and/or vision preparations needed to be positioned to launch a vision.
- ✓ If the member is ready, set measurable goals to work on establishing the foundation of the vision and in planting the vision.

Homework Explorations:

1. What are your thoughts regarding order?
2. What are your thoughts regarding protocol?
3. Study the scriptures listed in this chapter and share what you learned about having a healthy foundation. Journal your thoughts on the importance of the role of an apostle as it relates to having a solid foundation.
4. Ask God to show you areas within yourself that would be resistant to apostolic order and protocol. Journal where those issues stem from and spend time asking God to gut them out of your life. Journal your prayer experiences in this area.

KINGDOM ARMORBEARORS

By: Apostle Nina Cook, Vision Carrier, Kingdom Shifters Ministries, Muncie Indiana

Armor bearer derives from Greek language and literally means *"the one carrying the armor."* Biblically, they are known for helping a warrior carry their weapons into battle. An armor bearer would fight alongside the leading warrior in spite of many dangers and would help them in carrying out their strategic warfare plans against the enemy. They were dedicated soldiers that were exceptionally loyal and trustworthy. The position of armor bearer is one of great influence, as some of the top warriors listed amongst David's time were armor bearers. They are a source of protection and fortification for the person they are covering, and are skilled in war to combat the demonic forces that strive against the fulfillment of the assignment(s) of that leader and that leader themselves. They play a key role in the lives of frontline fivefold officers and have a grace to armor bearer the specific leader they are called to.

> **1Samuel 16:21** *And David came to Saul and entered his service. And Saul loved him greatly, and he became his armor-bearer.*
>
> **The Amplified Bible** *So David went to Saul and began serving him. Saul loved David very much, and David became his armor bearer.*

<u>Armor bearer in the *Strong's concordance* means:</u>
1. To lift, bear up, carry
2. To sustain, endure, support
3. To assist, bear continuously

David came to Saul and began to serve him. Saul loved David, and David became his armor bearer. His responsibility was elevated to lifting up, carrying, assisting, bearing consistently, enduring, and supporting Saul. We can assume from the scripture that because Saul loved David very much, that he felt a deep connection with David. This love then made room for David's elevation. At this time, I believe that Saul's love and heart for David was genuine. It is key that the leader- armor bearer relationship have a foundation of genuine love. This creates an atmosphere of trust and vulnerability for the leader to lean on the armor bearer and the armor bearer to fulfill all of the duties listed above and more. Both the armor bearer and leader should recognize this love and even engage it as they walk together and build this facet of their relationship. If this foundation of love is evident and acknowledged by both parties, the leader can be safe in knowing that the armor bearer will have their back and the armor bearer can be safe in knowing that they will not be taken advantage of or mistreated. The leader and the armor bearer will have to make sure to continually cultivate the fruit of love as they go throughout different seasons and grow together through the years. It is important that they not allow the hardships of the battles, their own personal issues, or attacks of the enemy set against their leader-armor bearer relationship to destroy them. Saul and David's relationship was destroyed when Saul allowed jealousy towards David to enter his heart.

> **1Samuel 18:7-9** *This was their song: "Saul has killed his thousands, and David his ten thousands!" This made Saul very angry. "What's this?" he said. "They credit David with ten thousands and me with only thousands. Next they'll be making him their king!" So from that time on Saul kept a jealous eye on David.*

This encounter quickly shifted the nature of their relationship from one of love to hate, rage, and made room for a murderous spirit to enter Saul's heart towards David. Leaders should never become upset when God rewards or blesses the armor bearer for their service and they must not see their armor bearer as a threat to who they are. They should be able to celebrate and honor their armor bearer for all that they do for them and the victories they gain for the kingdom of God as a whole. The leader and armor bearer should take time to refresh the genuine love that they have for one another, celebrate and honor one another and make sure to close their personal relationship off from the attack of the enemy. The power of this relationship is so demonstrative to the enemy that he will try anything to bring division to it and destroy it altogether. He knows that if he can divide the leader and armor bearer, the assignments ahead and each of them will be exposed and susceptible to attack. We must not give room to the enemy in this manner and make sure that love reigns in the relationship no matter the time or season.

I believe that there are different kinds of armor bearers. There are some that are called to serve just for a specific season, some that serve just as God unction's, some that serve for certain events and ministry assignments, some that serve in prayer covering or prophesy only, some that serve when asked to cover a leader for an assignment, and some that serve as lifestyle armor bearers that know they are walking closely with a specific leader through their life journey. No matter which kind, the armor bearer should always be skilled and effective in fulfilling their armor bearing duty.

David was called to be Saul's armor bearer for a specific season and he served and honored him with his life. God had a plan to elevate David into kingship and his armor bearer position helped to prepare and develop him into the king that he needed to be. There is great inheritance for those who serve. *Matthew 23:11* states, *"The greatest among you must be a servant."* Servanthood will always precede an elevation into greatness. There is a blessing and purpose for your armor bearing assignment. If you are an armor bearer, you should seek God for what that purpose is. Knowing the purpose will make you that much more effective as an armor bearer and in your own personal development of what you are to learn and receive from the leader you are serving.

Unfortunately, Saul turned on David, became jealous of him and aimed to kill him on multiple occasions. In spite of, David honorably and faithfully served the king and then he became the king. This was a part of his inheritance and reward. Armor bearers must faithfully serve in order to reach greatness in their own lives and callings. In many instances, depending on the call and plan of God for their lives, they will inherit and be elevated into governing rule over that which they have served. As you serve as an armor bearer, do not separate yourself from the assignment or have the mindset that you are serving the person just for them and their vision. You must shift to embracing your position as a part of who you are, who you are becoming, and realize that you are a part of the vision you are serving.

> *1Samuel 16:10-11* *And Jesse made seven of his sons pass before Samuel. And Samuel said to Jesse, "The Lord has not chosen these." Then Samuel said to Jesse, "Are all your sons here?" And he said, "There remains yet the youngest, but behold, he is keeping the sheep." And Samuel said to Jesse, "Send and get him, for we will not sit down till he comes here."*

Servanthood was a part of David's nature. Even before serving Saul, he was a servant. He served God in being a man after his own heart and he served his father Jesse and family in being responsible for tending the sheep. He was the greatest of all his brothers and he was found serving.

Armor bearers must FIRST and FOREMOST be servants. The suffix of hood on the word servanthood denotes the state, condition, character, class, or nature of a person or group of people. Servanthood is a condition and state of being. It should be a part of the nature and character of armor bearers. They must always be found serving and look for opportunities to serve. I am always identifying needs and taking the initiative to meet them. When I shifted into being an official armor bearer, my heart was already devoted to serving God, and I was naturally serving my leader and ministry. It was evident to her and even to the onlooker at times, that I was a servant leader. She recognized how I was serving her and how no one had ever done the things I was doing before. She shared her observations with me and we began to search this out deeper before the Lord. God revealed to her that I was to be her armor bearer. I would serve as her armor bearer throughout her apostolic journey and I was a part of her heritage and legacy. There would be great inheritance, reward and blessing for me in who God has called me to be that connected to her and the ministry as a whole.

As an armor bearer, you do not serve how you would want to be served, but how they would want to be served.

I believe that God reveals who an armor bearer is to the leader and armor bearer and that the timing of this revelation will be filled with purpose. I have been serving as an armor bearer to my leader for about six years now and I was revealed as her armor bearer on the brink of a great shift and transition in her life. I was also in the midst of a great shift and was aligning my life to walk in my God ordained destiny and live a life that was totally sold out to him and his call on my life. God knew that she would need the protection, support, and help in war that was coming her way as she elevated to the next dimension in her apostolic journey. And God knew that I needed an even greater deposit and impartation of what she had and who she was by serving as her armor bearer. Remember that serving always precedes a shift into greatness. I was handpicked for the job for a specific season in time in which I was needed the most and in which she was needed the most in my life.

Armor bearers should be handpicked by God. Although they will not be perfect and will have to learn many things on the job as they walk with their leader, they will have a unique grace, skill, effective power, and keenness to protect and serve. I say they will have to learn on the job because their armor bearing skill will become increasingly effectual as they walk with the leader and learn more about who they are in God, who they are personally, and what their God ordained destiny and assignment is. Initially, this takes time. When I first became an armor bearer, I had to learn a lot about my leader from this new perspective. Many armor bearing qualities came very natural to me. I would pray for her without her telling me to, I could recognize when things were wrong, I could see when she needed extra support. However, these things needed to be fine-tuned and I had to shift up higher in fulfilling this role in her life. As I was shifted into the role of her armor bearer, I had to learn her at a whole new dimension. Getting to really know the person you are serving is essential for an armor bearer. You can be serving someone and giving to them as best you know how, with all of your heart and with the best of your intentions, but if it is not their language it will not encourage and strengthen them in the specific way that they need for their life and calling. I had to learn her language and how to serve her in the unique way that she needed to be served. As an armor bearer, you do not serve how you would want to be served, but how they would want to be served.

This requires relationship and the development of a connection with that person. It is not only the job of the armor bearer to protect and war with their leader but to be able to support, lift them up and carry them at times as well. You have to really know them in order to do this effectively. If you do not have relationship, how will you come to know that person and understand their language and unspoken needs? How will you know what they are going through, what kinds of attacks they are experiencing, what God has been showing and speaking to them, what their weaknesses and strengths are, what they need help with and so on and so forth? Serving as an armor bearer is a very intimate position because the person you are serving has to be able to trust you with their life, share things with you that others may not know and to help them in protecting the fulfillment of their God- ordained vision.

When I first became an armor bearer, I was very attentive to my leader. Armor bearers must be attentive. This means that you are alert, aware and vigilant. This attentive posture greatly sharpened me as an armor bearer and allowed me to learn her very quickly. Proximity was important. So, when I would be around her, I would be watchful of what she said and shared with me, how she did things, how she prayed, how she prepared herself for ministry and more. I would come over to her house to spend time in prayer, help her clean, help her pack for out of town ministry engagements and etc. Due to me using that time to learn and be attentive, I learned how to do those things for her on my own where I did not need her assistance and I knew how to do them to her liking. Armor bearers should make things easier for those they serve. I learned how to help her in any way that I could which gave her more time to write, pray, prepare and stay closed in so that petty warfare attacks could not infiltrate. I was able to take some things off of her hands and even cover her as I did those things.

As I grew in relationship as an armor bearer, I had to learn how to break out of the fears of what she would think of me, getting it wrong, my prayers not being effective, or seeming like a disturbance to her. I initially struggled in these areas and in finding the right timing to do what I felt God leading me to do. If she was very quiet and working on writing a book but I sensed something, I would be fearful of interrupting her. In times where I would come into her home to help and she would be praying, I would wonder what I should do and how I could help. My confidence and boldness had to shift. I had to learn how to assert myself in my position and not be worried about whether I would be received or not. Armor bearers must not be fearful but confident and bold. If you feel you need a shift in this area, it is ok to pray about these things and decree confidence and boldness over yourself. When I began to no longer fear, I saw great fruit in what I did as her armor bearer. When she would pray, I would pray and even take over the prayer so she could reserve her energy. Even if she was quiet, I would share what the Lord gave me in good timing and pray for her. I realized that I was not a disturbance but a blessing. I was not an outside entity but a part of the process within itself. Now, I do not worry about these things at all. I am keen in knowing when to pray, when to share and when to be quiet because through attentive observation, I have mastered her language and know her hidden cues.

I became very observant to the point that I would know what was needed before she did. She would be looking for a mic or searching for her phone and I would be right there standing next to her already holding it. I could look at her and know that we needed to stop whatever we were doing and pray. I came to know when she needed more encouragement and support and I understood how to provide this. I began to notice patterns in the attacks that the enemy used against her and I gained much strategy on how to pray and what to pray to be effective. My ability to be keen and efficient in serving her continues to grow and evolve. I never get to a place of familiarity with my leader where I feel as if I know everything about her. I continue to posture myself to learn more about who she is and what she expands into. Since she does not stay the same, I must not stay the same. Just like with any other ministry operation, you never arrive and reach a place of perfection. Armor bearers have to be ok to evolve. They must be constant learners and flexible to shift with the seasons as their leaders change and as their ministries and mandates expand.

Armor bearers must guard themselves from familiarity. Especially if the leader- armor bearer have other relationship dynamics as well. My leader is also my spiritual mother, my mentor, my apostle, and my friend. I am also her spiritual daughter, governing successor and friend. When I am armor bearing, my focus is always on this one dynamic. I do not try to have mother- daughter or friend type conversations with her. I do not bring up things that are unrelated to the ministry at hand. I do not try to draw her away from what God has her focused on to engage in the other dynamics of our relationship. When I am on duty, I am on duty and I respect that. I do not take offense if she is quiet, does not talk much, and is completely focused on what God has granted to her hands at that time. I give her room to do that while covering her through prayer or whatever else may need to be done. Armor bearers must be able to interchange between relationship dynamics and not become familiar. If you give way to familiarity, this can be an open door to petty offenses, the crossing of boundaries, loss of respect, lack of honor and etc. Familiarity can easily make the armor bearer become careless, lax, put their guard down, can diminish the armor bearers ability to serve the leader effectively and can breach the relationship altogether. Armor bearers must keep themselves postured in humility and meekness so their character can remain intact to serve from a pure heart and spirit. This will keep them submitted to God, their leaders, and their armor bearer position. Humility kills familiarity.

I am a lifestyle armor bearer, so I will be speaking from this perspective. However, any kind of armor bearer can take keys from these points. As a lifestyle armor bearer, I do not serve seasonally or only for certain assignments. I armor bearer my leader in life and can be called on at any moment to pray, cover, help, or serve in any capacity. Armor bearers must possess the quality of selflessness. It must be their nature to put the needs of that leader before themselves. I often joke around and say that I am on call every day. I am always checking on my leader, asking if there are things that need to be done, praying for her, and the list goes on. I treat this position like I would any other job and take it very seriously because I know who I am spiritually and the effectiveness of my position. I cannot risk not being on my post and giving the enemy room to find a foothold. Some would look at me and say "you do too much," however, if they knew the level of attack and warfare that we experience, they would understand why she needs to be covered with such intensity. Another person may not need the same thing, but I know what is needed as it pertains to my armor bearing responsibility. As an armor bearer, you must know what is necessary for you to fulfill your specific job.

I know that I thwart the assignments of hell set against her and keep her uplifted. My leader is an apostle and the career of an apostle is one of warfare, so I always have to be in position to not only defend but to be offensive against the enemy. When attacks do infiltrate, I have a grace to produce breakthrough, deliverance, and to keep persevering with her to wholeness. You have to be selfless in order to serve in this way continually. I will say from my personal experience that as an armor bearer, God will give you supernatural strength and the ability to push through in serving even when you are tired. There have been times where I felt tired and as soon as I began to pray and cover my leader, I felt a strength and power that I did not have before. I knew that was God's grace being made perfect in my weakness. There is a grace, supernatural power and strength within the position itself, but you have to be actively operating in the position to tap into it. If he calls you to such a level of selflessness and sacrifice, trust him to provide you with everything you need to sustain and maintain in it. You can also trust him to give you times of rest and refreshing. **Proverbs 11:25** says *"Generous persons will prosper; those who refresh others will themselves be refreshed."* As armor bearers serve selflessly, they can rest assured that they themselves will be refreshed.

I serve as a resource of protection, fortification and encouragement for my leader. She knows that she can call on me whether it is the middle of the day or the middle of the night. I act as a place of safety and even a vault as a keeper of secrets for her. There must be a confidentiality agreement between the leader- armor bearer, such that delicate information can be shared and the leader can trust that it will not come out of the vault of the relationship. Other people may mishandle the information and at any point could turn and use the information against the leader. Therefore, the information must be handled with care. The leader can share various things with the armor bearer about how they are being attacked, personal life and family challenges, psychological warfare issues, that they are feeling depressed and are thinking about quitting the ministry and so on. The leader must be assured that the armor bearer will not breach the relationship and spread their hardships around, but that they will be there to partner with them in breaking through these challenging times.

When my leader shares personal information with me, that information never gets out. I serve as a source of strength to her even if I just provide a listening ear. There are times when I might share encouraging words, I might search the challenge out before the Lord to receive a solution or word, I might pray immediately, I might give her a hug and surround her with love, I might bring her some breakfast and Starbucks (her favorite) to cheer her up, or I might just listen and sit with her. As an armor bearer, it is ok to not have an answer to everything. This does not make you a bad armor bearer, it just makes you human. Armor bearer, you are NOT God. It is important for armor bearers to remember this and reposition themselves as a vessel being used by God and not God themselves. There was a time in my armor bearing experience where I became a fixer and I would be very sad and depressed when I could not fix whatever it was that my leader was going through. When she would get sick, I would be heart broken and angry with the devil. This even progressed to the point where there would be times, I was mad at God and I would desperately ask him "why does she keep getting sick when she does so much for you." I would have times of crying when I would be alone and instead of being able to get a prayer through, I was all caught up in my emotions when I should have been pushing in the spirit. Armor bearers must know how to balance their emotions and their spirit. Due to such intimate close relation in the leader- armor bearer relationship, there will be a great depth of love that the two will share. We already discussed how the foundation of the relationship is one of genuine love. This love has to be balanced and emotions often have to put aside in order to stay spiritually grounded and effective as an armor bearer. I had to learn how to rise up above being sad that she was sick and being attacked and press into blasting demons and hell with my prayers to help break her through. My prayers and my position as her armor bearer was a source of healing and deliverance for her, so I had to learn how to stay on my post. We are human, so of course there will be times where you will get mad at the devil and feel sad when someone is hurt. However, the key is not to stay there. You have to shift up out of that and ascend into the third heavens so that you create a solution to the problem.

As an armor bearer, you will need to make sure to take time to cleanse and heal personally especially after seasons of intense warfare. Often times, armor bearers take hits for their leader that they do not even recognize. This time is key so that warfare wounds can be healed and those hidden wounds can be exposed and healed as well. All soldiers need times of healing and restoration. When the next season of war begins, you will be healed, strengthened and ready to go back onto the battlefield and continue gaining victories. My leader is very sensitive to me. As much as I take care of her, she takes care of me. When she sees that I need prayer, she will pray for me. If she notices that I am having a moment of sadness, she will hug me. Leaders should make sure to care for their armor bearers. You need them to be at their best both spiritually and naturally. They are your most valuable soldiers.

I would like to take a moment to dispel some myths as it pertains to armor bearers. In my research on the position of an armor bearer, there was much question on whether it was biblical in today's church. Many articles concluded that it was not biblical and not necessary as the position of the armor bearer in the Old Testament was needed due to the physical nature of war and battle that the warriors engaged in. I even read articles that said the job of the armor bearer of the church today is to carry the bible of the pastor which is their sword. I was appalled at the lack of revelation and what was being presented about the modern day armor bearer. I was immediately led to the scripture, *Ephesians 6:12* where it states, "*For we wrestle not against flesh and blood, but against principalities, against powers, against the rulers of the darkness of this world, against spiritual wickedness in high places.*" The war that we are battling today is not against flesh and blood as it was in the times of the Old Testament. They were physically fighting against enemy armies for land, territory, jurisdiction, possession, people, generations, and the promises of God. In times today, the war is no longer in the realm of the natural, it is a spiritual war and our weapons are spiritual. This biblical revelation kills the argument that armor bearers are not needed today due to the change in war. We are indeed still in a battle but it is a different kind of battle. We no longer carry physical tangible weapons. The armor bearers of today carry spiritual weapons that are effective against the principalities and powers that we are currently battling against in this age. The war is in the realm of the spirit, so as

2Corinthians 10:4 states, *"For the weapons of our warfare are not carnal, but mighty through God to the pulling down of strongholds,"* our weapons are no longer of the flesh. This kills the argument that the job of the armor bearer is to carry the bible of their pastor, as this description of who they are still limits them to a physical tangible weapon that you can see. It also greatly diminishes the power and might of the armor bearer who biblically is known to be a fierce warrior that bodyguards the life of the person they are covering and slays all enemies concerning that person. From the Old Testament to the New Testament, how did the armor bearer go from being listed among the greatest of warriors to being a bible carrier? I conclude, that it is not so! Armor bearers have many weapons in the spirit that you may not be able to see that fight against the unseen forces to shield, protect, and even annihilate that which comes to attack and oppose the person they are covering. They are not bible carriers (although they can serve their leaders in this way but are not limited to) but warriors and mighty men and women of valor. Armor bearers are still very much alive today and are a much needed resource of protection, support and fortification for the frontline fivefold officers of today.

Qualities of an Effective Armor bearer:

- Armor bearers must be servants first and foremost.
- Armor bearers must be servant leaders.
- Armor bearers must walk in genuine love.
- Armor bearers must be selfless.
- Armor bearers must know their purpose.
- Armor bearers must be safe places.
- Armor bearers must be serious about their position and treat it just like any other job.
- Armor bearers must be offensive against the enemy and strategists.
- Armor bearers must be a resource of protection, fortification and encouragement.
- Armor bearers must not separate themselves from the assignment but know that they are a part of the vision they serve and have great inheritance and reward concerning it.
- Armor bearers must be attentive and watchful.
- Armor bearers must make things easier for their leaders.
- Armor bearers must be warriors skilled in spiritual warfare.
- Armor bearers must be vigilant in prayer and in fulfilling their duties.
- Armor bearers must be humble and meek and make sure to keep their character intact to serve effectively.

- Armor bearers must be persevering so that even in times of tiredness they can press into supernatural strength and power.
- Armor bearers must take time to cleanse and heal from warfare wounds.
- Armor bearers must be persevering so they can tap into the unique grace and supernatural strength that is within their position.
- Armor bearers must trust God to pour back into them and give them rest and refreshing.
- Armor bearers must balance their emotions and love for their leader with the spirit.
- Armor bearers must be faithful and loyal.
- Armor bearers must take initiative and not sit back and wait to be told what to do.
- Armor bearers must be sensitive, keen and discerning.
- Armor bearers must be bold and confident.
- Armor bearers must be learners and never feel as if they have arrived.
- Armor bearers must guard against familiarity with those they serve and never feel as if they know everything about that person.
- Armor bearers must be relational, encouraging and understanding.
- Armor bearers must be a vault and a keeper of secrets.
- Armor bearers must be keen and a discerner of times and seasons.
- Armor bearers must seek to be masters of the language of their leader.
- Armor bearers must be supportive and loving.
- Armor bearers must be flexible and able to evolve and grow with their leaders.
- Armor bearers must not be quick to take things personal and take offense.
- Armor bearers must not only identify needs but meet them.
- Armor bearers must not be fearful.
- Armor bearers must not stay the same but change as their leader changes.
- Armor bearers must not be fixers and put themselves in the position of God.
- Armor bearers must not mix other relationship dynamics into the time of armor bearing during ministry preparations and ministry itself.
- Armor bearers must not worry about what people think of them. They must know what they need to do to be effective in serving the

unique calling and mandate on their leaders' life and be unapologetic about it.
* **Armor bearers are still needed today!**

Homework Explorations:
1. What are some other qualities you believe an armor bearer should have?
2. Why do you think armor bearers are still needed today?
3. Why do you think it is important for the armor bearer not to get too familiar with their leader and in their position?
4. The foundation of the leader- armor bearer relationship must be one of genuine love, vulnerability, trust, intimate connection and confidentiality. Why do you believe these aspects are necessary to the relationship?
5. Take some time to journal on this subject and discuss what you learned regarding being an armor bearer.

ADMINISTRATING FIVEFOLD MINISTRY

By: Elder Amanda Barnhill, Vision Carrier of Kingdom Shifters Ministries
Muncie, Indiana

Administrators have been known in society as ones who assist in managing some of the clerical items for the upper management of an organization.

Dictionary.com defines *administer* as:
verb (used with object):
1. to manage (affairs, a government, etc.); have executive charge of
2. to bring into use or operation
3. to make application of; give
4. to supervise the formal taking of (an oath or the like)
5. Law. to manage or dispose of, as a decedent's estate by an executor or administrator or a trust estate by a trustee

verb (used without object):
1. to contribute assistance; bring aid or supplies (usually followed by to)
2. to perform the duties of an administrator

Dictionary.com defines an *administrator* as:
1. a person who manages or has a talent for managing
2. Law. a person appointed by a court to take charge of the estate of a decedent, but not appointed in the decedent's will

There are different levels of administration, but as an administrator, the focus is to assist in the success and full functioning of the ministry. Some of the attributes of an administrator are:

- ✓ Determination to accomplish the focus and goal of an assignment despite challenges or hardships.
- ✓ An Ox-Eagle anointing that rest upon the administrator to plow, plant, and build.
- ✓ The ability to take charge or take care of.
- ✓ The ability to influence or govern over.
- ✓ The ability to handle, direct, delegate, govern in actions and operation.
- ✓ The ability to see the bigger picture and plan ahead while still being present with what God is doing now.

- ✓ The ability to be trustworthy, dependable and reliable.
- ✓ The ability to operate in wisdom.
- ✓ The ability to be trained and to train others.
- ✓ The ability to have great faith.

The most common scripture known for administration is *1Corinthians 12:28*. It is a foundational piece in understanding the role of administration within a fivefold ministry and its importance to the body of Christ.

> *1Corinthians 12:28 And God hath set some in the church, first apostles, secondarily prophets, thirdly teachers, after that miracles, then gifts of healings, helps, governments, diversities of tongues.*

> *1Corinthians 12:28 New King James Bible And God has appointed these in the church: first apostles, second prophets, third teachers, after that miracles, then gifts of healings, helps, administrations, varieties of tongues.*

In this scripture, we see that God set not only fivefold offices but gifts as well in the church. Administration is a position that cannot be loosely appointed, but God must set the administrator. An administrator must be ordained by God for the vision and assignment of the fivefold team and the church.

According to Strong's to *set* means:
1. to put, laydown, make, appoint, kneel down, to set on(serve) something
2. to set forth, something to be explained by discourse
3. to make(or set) for one's self or one's use, to set, fix establish, to set forth
4. to establish and to ordain, to place (in the widest application
5. literally and figuratively; properly, in a passive or horizontal posture), advise, bow, commit, conceive, and give

When God has set a person as an administrator, total commitment to the vision, the ministry, and the team that God has positioned them with are key components to truly being operable in the full authority of an administrator. Notice that being operable in full authority comes with solidification of the administrator in the place that God has set them. What feels like limits may often times be a lack of commitment or submission. Explore those areas with God and allow him to heal the places in you that would limit the fullness of the administrator from coming forth.

An administrator must have a servant's heart and continuously be postured to assist with carrying the vision in various aspects. A true administrator must learn to lay down their lives and continuously cast down spirits of pride and rejection so that they can be positioned to conceive, carry, nurture, and govern the vision, ministry, and team that God has set them in.

As we continue to explore **1Corinthians 12:28**, let's look at the meaning of administration (or governments in KJV) as well as helps.

Strong's definition for *government* is *kybérnēsis*:
1. pilotage, i.e. (figuratively) directorship (in the church): — government

Strong's definition of *helps* is *antílēpsis*:
1. relief: — help
2. to take hold of in turn, i.e. succor; also to participate: — help, partaker, support

The gift of administration and the gift of helps become intertwined when one is an administrator, but the assignments are different. Within a fivefold ministry, the administrator will operate with the gift of helps and bring relief and assistance where needed. However, one who has the gift of helps is not always one who is an administrator. The gift of helps is to assist with relief, aid, and assistance, while the purpose of an administrator in the fivefold ministry is to represent fivefold mandate and vision while guiding, governing, setting order, and managing the implementation of the vision of the ministry through the direction of the Apostle. This is why it is so essential for administrators to have a servant's heart. In various seasons, the administrator may be assisting and bringing relief to the fivefold team so that they are able to focus on their particular assignment. This particularly happens with small teams, but as an administrator, the heart is to carry the vision and implement the directions laid out by the Apostle, and sometimes that includes doing anything that is needed. This is also why submitting to the vision and committing to where God has placed the administrator is essential as it is not always glamorous but a submitted and committed heart will do what needs to be done no matter the various seasons.

Within a fivefold ministry team, each office governs within its jurisdiction but works together to equip and empower the body of Christ in their identities and destinies. Each officer is a leader in their own right. As the administrator, the assignment is to listen to the heart of each officer, while maintaining the instructions of the Apostle, and assist them in the success, execution, and implementation of their piece of the vision.

As an armor bearer, you do not serve how you would want to be served, but how they would want to be served.

The requirements and duties of an administrator:

There are specific requirements for being set as an administrator. The ability to be trusted with the vision and carry the vision is essential to the ministry being able to expand, develop, teach, train and occupy. It allows the mandate and assignment of the ministry to be the focus of the leader. This can be very simple and yet very complex all in the same breath. As an administrator, good character is required in order to be set and truly operate in the position of an administrator. I am not saying that someone is not an administrator if they struggle in their character. I am saying that they do have to be willing to be processed in their character so that the full authority of an administrator can come forth. *Acts 6:1-7* is a good example of character required by an administrator.

> *Acts 6:1-7 And in those days, when the number of the disciples was multiplied, there arose a murmuring of the Grecians against Hebrews, because their widows were neglected in the daily ministration. Then the twelve called the multitude of the disciples unto them, and said, It is not reason that we should leave the word of God, and serve tables. Wherefore, brethren, look ye out among you seven men of honest report, full of the Holy Ghost and wisdom, whom we may appoint over this business. But we will give ourselves continually to prayer, and to the ministry of the word. And the saying pleased the whole multitude: and they chose Stephen, a man full of faith and of the Holy Ghost, and Philip, and Prochorus, and Nicanor, and Timon, and Parmenas, and Nicolas a proselyte of Antioch: Whom they set before the apostles: and when they had prayed, they laid their hands on them. And the word of God increased; and the number of the disciples multiplied in Jerusalem greatly; and a great company of the priests were obedient to the faith.*

Acts 6:1-7 Easy-to-Read Bible More and more people were becoming followers of Jesus. But during this same time, Greek-speaking followers began to complain against the other Jewish followers. They said that their widows were not getting their share of what the followers received every day. The twelve apostles called the whole group of followers together. The apostles said to them, "It would not be right for us to give up our work of teaching God's word in order to be in charge of getting food to people. So, brothers and sisters, choose seven of your men who have a good reputation. They must be full of wisdom and the Spirit. We will give them this work to do. Then we can use all our time to pray and to teach the word of God." The whole group liked the idea. So they chose these seven men: Stephen (a man with great faith and full of the Holy Spirit), Philip,[a]Prochorus, Nicanor, Timon, Parmenas, and Nicolaus (a man from Antioch who had become a Jew). Then they put these men before the apostles, who prayed and laid their hands on them. The word of God was reaching more and more people. The group of followers in Jerusalem became larger and larger. Even a big group of Jewish priests believed and obeyed.

Honest Report

As the seven were chosen, the requirements and expectations were clearly laid out. Those who were to be set in the position had to be ones that were publicly recognized by the multitude as reliable, as someone that they respect, as someone who is full of the Holy Spirit (operating in the fullness of Christ that lives within), as someone who is a skilled expert, cultivated, learned, and clearly shows that they carry the wisdom of God in forming and executing in the government of the world and scriptures. This is the character of the administrator. Within a fivefold ministry team, the administrator's dependability is vital to the execution of the mandate. The team that God has set the administrator in needs to be able to trust them to implement and execute even when they are not looking. The team has to be able to trust that they can depend on the administrator and can have some relief so that they can focus on a particular assignment and mandate. Lack of dependability could mean that an assignment that has been given to the leader is not being provided the full attention needed because they are working on things that the administrator could be doing to assist them.

Full of the Holy Spirit

An administrator will learn quickly that the Holy Spirit will teach, guide, and direct with strategy when they are positioned in the right place with the right posture. A personal example of this in our ministry would be the development of self-published books. When Apostle Taquetta started writing books, she would ask me how to do certain task in Microsoft Word that to be honest, I had absolutely, positively no idea how to do. All I knew was that she had a great deal to offer the world and anything I could do to make sure that message got out in the spirit of excellence that she operates in, I would. So, I researched, I googled, I took classes, and yes I used YouTube (do not sleep on it). I became skilled and cultivated in order to assist in the production of books. There are some areas in the process that are not my expertise, but the bonus of working with and walking with a fivefold ministry team is that I do not have to be a one-man show. I can simply be my piece, and the work will still be completed in the excellence that has been instructed by my Apostle.

Full of wisdom

Administrators are governmental. They handle the business side of things but with a kingdom mindset. This can include handling finances, taxes, other business affairs, and clerical duties. It can also include other modes of assistance and operating in the gift of helps. Ultimately, administrators have to embody the heart of a servant and help where needed in order to implement and execute the vision and assignment of the ministry. They have the capacity to handle and serve God and his people by leading various affairs in the ministry and vision. They search out a strategy for how to implement and execute the instruction of the leader. When operating in a fivefold team, the administrator will begin to see where the ministry is going and begin to prepare for it. They also grow into learning to see the bigger picture so that they can assist the leader in carrying the weight, preparing the team and those connected with the ministry, for the order and structure of the ministry as well as where they are going as a unit.

It can be a challenge to learn the balance of what the administrator is seeing for where the ministry and team is going and where the unit is now. This is where learning to steer the ship takes place, and the need to truly walk with and listen to the instructions of the leader is vital. When being positioned as an administrator, you are being trusted by God and your leader to help steer the vision. It is important for the administrator to communicate with the leader and be clear on the vision and what the leader needs from them in that season or time. The ability to walk with the leader at this capacity is an honor and also a training ground for another shift in leadership and identity. The ability to truly receive all that God is working out in and through them depends on the administrator's ability to submit and commit to the leader, the process, the training ground, what God is speaking for them, and embracing all that is being released to the administrator.

The sent administrator

There are times the administrator will be sent on behalf of the leader to execute the assignment. In Titus 1, we see that the Apostle Paul leaves Titus in charge of Crete to complete the work that he had started. He gave Titus instructions to appoint leaders based off his guidelines. Apostle Paul gave him tools to aid him in establishing good leaders and implementing the full vision.

> ***Titus 1*** *Paul, a servant of God, and an apostle of Jesus Christ, according to the faith of God's elect, and the acknowledging of the truth which is after godliness; In hope of eternal life, which God, that cannot lie, promised before the world began; But hath in due times manifested his word through preaching, which is committed unto me according to the commandment of God our Saviour; To Titus, mine own son after the common faith: Grace, mercy, and peace, from God the Father and the Lord Jesus Christ our Saviour. For this cause left I thee in Crete, that thou shouldest set in order the things that are wanting, and ordain elders in every city, as I had appointed thee: If any be blameless, the husband of one wife, having faithful children not accused of riot or unruly. For a bishop must be blameless, as the steward of God; not selfwilled, not soon angry, not given to wine, no striker, not given to filthy lucre; But a lover of hospitality, a lover of good men, sober, just, holy, temperate; Holding fast the faithful word as he hath been taught, that he may be able by sound doctrine both to exhort and to convince the gainsayers. For there are many unruly and vain talkers and deceivers, specially they of the circumcision: Whose mouths must be stopped, who subvert whole houses, teaching things which they ought not, for filthy lucre's sake. One of themselves, even a prophet of their own, said, the Cretians are alway liars, evil beasts, slow bellies. This witness is true. Wherefore rebuke them sharply, that they may be sound in the faith; Not giving heed to Jewish fables, and commandments of men, that turn from the truth. Unto the pure all things are pure: but unto them that are defiled and unbelieving is nothing pure; but even their mind and conscience is defiled. They profess that they know God; but in works they deny him, being abominable, and disobedient, and unto every good work reprobate.*

> ***Titus 1 The Message Bible*** *I, Paul, am God's slave and Christ's agent for promoting the faith among God's chosen people, getting out the accurate word on God and how to respond rightly to it. My aim is to raise hopes by pointing the way to life without end. This is the life God promised long ago — and he doesn't break promises! And then when the time was ripe, he went public with his truth. I've been entrusted to proclaim this Message by order of our Savior, God himself. Dear Titus, legitimate son in the faith: Receive everything God our Father and Jesus our Savior give you! I left you in charge in Crete so you could complete what I left half-done. Appoint leaders in every town according to my instructions. As you select them, ask, "Is this man well-thought-of? Is he committed to his wife? Are his children believers? Do they respect him and stay out of trouble?" It's important that a church leader, responsible for the affairs in God's house, be looked up to — not pushy, not short-tempered, not a drunk, not a bully, not money-hungry. He must welcome people, be helpful, wise, fair, reverent, have a good grip on himself, and have a good grip on the Message, knowing how to use the truth to either spur people on in knowledge or stop them in their tracks if they oppose it. For there are a lot of rebels out there, full of loose, confusing, and deceiving talk. Those who were brought up religious and ought to know better are the worst. They've got to be shut up. They're disrupting entire families with their teaching, and all for the sake of a fast buck. One of their own prophets said it best: The Cretans are liars from the womb, barking dogs, lazy bellies. He certainly spoke the truth. Get on them right away. Stop that diseased talk of Jewish make-believe and made-up rules so they can recover a robust faith. Everything is clean to the clean-minded; nothing is clean to dirty-minded unbelievers. They leave their dirty fingerprints on every thought and act. They say they know God, but their actions speak louder than their words. They're real creeps, disobedient good-for-nothings.*

Another example of an administrator being sent on behalf of a fivefold leader is when Baruch was sent on behalf of Jeremiah to the temple to declare a word from the Lord.

> ***Jeremiah 36:4-8*** *Then Jeremiah called Baruch the son of Neriah: and Baruch wrote from the mouth of Jeremiah all the words of the Lord, which he had spoken unto him, upon a roll of a book. And Jeremiah commanded Baruch, saying, I am shut up; I cannot go into the house of the Lord: Therefore go thou, and read in the roll, which thou hast written from my mouth, the words of the Lord in the ears of the people in the Lord's house upon the fasting day: and also thou shalt read them in the ears of all Judah*

that come out of their cities. It may be they will present their supplication before the Lord, and will return every one from his evil way: for great is the anger and the fury that the Lord hath pronounced against this people. And Baruch the son of Neriah did according to all that Jeremiah the prophet commanded him, reading in the book the words of the Lord in the Lord's house.

Jeremiah 36:4-8 The Message Bible *So Jeremiah called in Baruch son of Neriah. Jeremiah dictated and Baruch wrote down on a scroll everything that God had said to him. Then Jeremiah told Baruch, "I'm blacklisted. I can't go into God's Temple, so you'll have to go in my place. Go into the Temple and read everything you've written at my dictation. Wait for a day of fasting when everyone is there to hear you. And make sure that all the people who come from the Judean villages hear you. "Maybe, just maybe, they'll start praying and God will hear their prayers. Maybe they'll turn back from their bad lives. This is no light matter. God has certainly let them know how angry he is!" Baruch son of Neriah did everything Jeremiah the prophet told him to do. In the Temple of God he read the Message of God from the scroll.*

Administrators carry the anointings of the fivefold ministry team leaders. This allows the administrator to assist the leader in executing their piece of the vision mandate. Administrators have to maintain a posture of being open and submitted to operating in various capacities and not limit or box themselves in as their operations are based on the anointing, mantle, mandate and purpose of the vision that they have been set in.

The time management of the administrator
Time management and wisdom go hand in hand for the administrator. Wisdom allows the administrator to make the best use of their time. When working with a fivefold team, the administrator can go from having all duties completed to everyone needing assistance. The mandate of the fivefold team can cause great acceleration, and keeping up with the momentum is vital for the administrator to be able to operate with the team fully. This means the administrator cannot procrastinate and must tap into wisdom to gain strategy on how to balance the vision that God has set them in.

> ***Ephesians 5:15-17*** *See then that ye walk circumspectly, not as fools, but as wise, Redeeming the time, because the days are evil. Wherefore be ye not unwise, but understanding what the will of the Lord is.*

> *Ephesians 5:15-17 The Amplified Bible Therefore see that you walk carefully [living life with honor, purpose, and courage; shunning those who tolerate and enable evil], not as the unwise, but as wise [sensible, intelligent, discerning people], making the very most of your time [on earth, recognizing and taking advantage of each opportunity and using it with wisdom and diligence], because the days are [filled with] evil. Therefore do not be foolish and thoughtless, but understand and firmly grasp what the will of the Lord is.*

The SHIFT from student to leader

As we continue to grow in God's character, nature, and his carefully crafted blueprint for our lives, we will always be learning, but there is a point of maturity where we shift to the ability to lead.

> *Acts 6:1-7 And in those days, when the number of the disciples was multiplied, there arose a murmuring of the Grecians against Hebrews, because their widows were neglected in the daily ministration. Then the twelve called the multitude of the disciples unto them, and said, It is not reason that we should leave the word of God, and serve tables. Wherefore, brethren, look ye out among you seven men of honest report, full of the Holy Ghost and wisdom, whom we may appoint over this business. But we will give ourselves continually to prayer, and to the ministry of the word. And the saying pleased the whole multitude: and they chose Stephen, a man full of faith and of the Holy Ghost, and Philip, and Prochorus, and Nicanor, and Timon, and Parmenas, and Nicolas a proselyte of Antioch: Whom they set before the apostles: and when they had prayed, they laid their hands on them. And the word of God increased; and the number of the disciples multiplied in Jerusalem greatly; and a great company of the priests were obedient to the faith.*

In this scripture, we see that as the 12 continued to share the gospel, the number of disciples continued to grow. As the community or team began to grow, there was an area that needed some attention, structure and governance. The 12 needed to remain focused on their mandate, so they told the multitude of disciples to choose seven from among themselves that they felt were ready to be put in a position to lead.

Disciples in Greek is *mathētés* and means, *"a learner, i.e. pupil, disciple."*

One key in this scripture is that administrators have a process. There is a season of learning, being a student, and one who follows. In order to become skilled and become solidified in identity, there is a season of following, being taught, and studying to show themselves approved. There is a season of learning to grow in character, in skill, in maturity, in gifts, and in callings. There is a season of learning God's voice and building relationship with him. Then there comes a season where those areas become mature, and it is time to shift from the pupil to the leader. Administrators are constantly learning, but the mindset of being a pupil only must shift. An embracing of the maturity and stepping into the fullness of the identity of the administrator must take place or it will cause a stagnancy in the momentum of the operation of the mantle on their lives and the blessing and purpose for which they have been set within a fivefold team. Administrators embrace both the ability to follow and to rise up as a leader as they come into full maturity of the shift that God, their leader, and their team are calling for in that season.

Homework Explorations:
1. What are the requirements of an administrator?
    a. What areas do you need to improve to fully shift into operating as an administrator?
2. What posture should the administrator have?
    a. What areas of resistance keep the administrator from this posture continually?
3. What role does the administrator play in the fivefold team dynamic within your ministry?
4. What season of their process is the administrator in?
    a. What ways can the team assist them in their process?

THE NECESSITY OF SUCCESSORS

Successors are vital to the vision being established and advanced in the earth and being SHIFTED from generation to generation.

Jesus & The Disciples
The disciples actually walked with Jesus and everything he did was preparing and aligning them as successors.

> *Matthew 4:19-20 And he saith unto them, Follow me, and I will make you fishers of men. And they straightway left their nets, and followed him.*
>
> *Mathew 9:37-38 Then saith he unto his disciples, The harvest truly is plenteous, but the labourers are few; Pray ye therefore the Lord of the harvest, that he will send forth labourers into his harvest.*
>
> *Matthew 10:6-16 But go rather to the lost sheep of the house of Israel. And as ye go, preach, saying, The kingdom of heaven is at hand. Heal the sick, cleanse the lepers, raise the dead, cast out devils: freely ye have received, freely give. Provide neither gold, nor silver, nor brass in your purses, Nor scrip for your journey, neither two coats, neither shoes, nor yet staves: for the workman is worthy of his meat. And into whatsoever city or town ye shall enter, enquire who in it is worthy; and there abide till ye go thence. And when ye come into an house, salute it. And if the house be worthy, let your peace come upon it: but if it be not worthy, let your peace return to you. And whosoever shall not receive you, nor hear your words, when ye depart out of that house or city, shake off the dust of your feet. Verily I say unto you, It shall be more tolerable for the land of Sodom and Gomorrha in the day of judgment, than for that city. Behold, I send you forth as sheep in the midst of wolves: be ye therefore wise as serpents, and harmless as doves.*
>
> *Luke 6:13-23 And when it was day, he called unto him his disciples: and of them he chose twelve, whom also he named apostles; Simon, (whom he also named Peter,) and Andrew his brother, James and John, Philip and Bartholomew, Matthew and Thomas, James the son of Alphaeus, and Simon called Zelotes, And Judas the brother of James, and Judas Iscariot, which also was the traitor.*
> *And he came down with them, and stood in the plain, and the company of his disciples, and a great multitude of people out of all Judaea and*

Jerusalem, and from the sea coast of Tyre and Sidon, which came to hear him, and to be healed of their diseases; And they that were vexed with unclean spirits: and they were healed. And the whole multitude sought to touch him: for there went virtue out of him, and healed them all.

And he lifted up his eyes on his disciples, and said, Blessed be ye poor: for yours is the kingdom of God. Blessed are ye that hunger now: for ye shall be filled. Blessed are ye that weep now: for ye shall laugh. Blessed are ye, when men shall hate you, and when they shall separate you from their company, and shall reproach you, and cast out your name as evil, for the Son of man's sake. Rejoice ye in that day, and leap for joy: for, behold, your reward is great in heaven: for in the like manner did their fathers unto the prophets.

Luke 9:1-6 *Then he called his twelve disciples together, and gave them power and authority over all devils, and to cure diseases. And he sent them to preach the kingdom of God, and to heal the sick. And he said unto them, Take nothing for your journey, neither staves, nor scrip, neither bread, neither money; neither have two coats apiece. And whatsoever house ye enter into, there abide, and thence depart. And whosoever will not receive you, when ye go out of that city, shake off the very dust from your feet for a testimony against them. And they departed, and went through the towns, preaching the gospel, and healing every where.*

John 14:12 *Verily, verily, I say unto you, He that believeth on me, the works that I do shall he do also; and greater works than these shall he do; because I go unto my Father.*

John 16:12-16 *I have yet many things to say unto you, but ye cannot bear them now. Howbeit when he, the Spirit of truth, is come, he will guide you into all truth: for he shall not speak of himself; but whatsoever he shall hear, that shall he speak: and he will shew you things to come. He shall glorify me: for he shall receive of mine, and shall shew it unto you. All things that the Father hath are mine: therefore said I, that he shall take of mine, and shall shew it unto you. A little while, and ye shall not see me: and again, a little while, and ye shall see me, because I go to the Father.*

John 13:34-35 *A new commandment I give to you, that you love one another: just as I have loved you, you also are to love one another. By this all people will know that you are my disciples, if you have love for one another."*

***John 15:18-21 English Standard Bible** If the world hates you, know that it has hated me before it hated you. If you were of the world, the world would love you as its own; but because you are not of the world, but I chose you out of the world, therefore the world hates you. Remember the word that I said to you: 'A servant is not greater than his master.' If they persecuted me, they will also persecute you. If they kept my word, they will also keep yours. But all these things they will do to you on account of my name, because they do not know him who sent me.*
***Acts 1:8** But ye shall receive power, after that the Holy Ghost is come upon you: and ye shall be witnesses unto me both in Jerusalem, and in all Judaea, and in Samaria, and unto the uttermost part of the earth.*

Paul & Timothy

Timothy walked in ministry with Paul. Paul also was preparing and aligning him as a successor. Timothy was already a successor of his grandmother's ministry. He carried two legacies to the next generation (***Study 1st and 2nd Timothy***).

***Acts 16:1-5** Then came he to Derbe and Lystra: and, behold, a certain disciple was there, named Timotheus, the son of a certain woman, which was a Jewess, and believed; but his father was a Greek: Which was well reported of by the brethren that were at Lystra and Iconium. Him would Paul have to go forth with him; and took and circumcised him because of the Jews which were in those quarters: for they knew all that his father was a Greek. And as they went through the cities, they delivered them the decrees for to keep, that were ordained of the apostles and elders which were at Jerusalem. And so were the churches established in the faith, and increased in number daily.*

***1Timothy 1:1-7** Paul, an apostle of Jesus Christ by the commandment of God our Saviour, and Lord Jesus Christ, which is our hope; Unto Timothy, my own son in the faith: Grace, mercy, and peace, from God our Father and Jesus Christ our Lord. As I besought thee to abide still at Ephesus, when I went into Macedonia, that thou mightest charge some that they teach no other doctrine, Neither give heed to fables and endless genealogies, which minister questions, rather than godly edifying which is in faith: so do. Now the end of the commandment is charity out of a pure heart, and of a good conscience, and of faith unfeigned: From which some having swerved have turned aside unto vain jangling; Desiring to be teachers of the law; understanding neither what they say, nor whereof they affirm.*

2Timothy 1:2-9 To Timothy, my dearly beloved son: Grace, mercy, and peace, from God the Father and Christ Jesus our Lord. I thank God, whom I serve from my forefathers with pure conscience, that without ceasing I have remembrance of thee in my prayers night and day; Greatly desiring to see thee, being mindful of thy tears, that I may be filled with joy; When I call to remembrance the unfeigned faith that is in thee, which dwelt first in thy grandmother Lois, and thy mother Eunice; and I am persuaded that in thee also. Wherefore I put thee in remembrance that thou stir up the gift of God, which is in thee by the putting on of my hands. For God hath not given us the spirit of fear; but of power, and of love, and of a sound mind.

Be not thou therefore ashamed of the testimony of our Lord, nor of me his prisoner: but be thou partaker of the afflictions of the gospel according to the power of God; Who hath saved us, and called us with an holy calling, not according to our works, but according to his own purpose and grace, which was given us in Christ Jesus before the world began.

1Timothy 1:18-19 *This charge I commit unto thee, son Timothy, according to the prophecies which went before on thee, that thou by them mightest war a good warfare. Holding faith, and a good conscience; which some having put away concerning faith have made shipwreck.*

1Timothy 4:12-16 *Let no man despise thy youth; but be thou an example of the believers, in word, in conversation, in charity, in spirit, in faith, in purity. Till I come, give attendance to reading, to exhortation, to doctrine. Neglect not the gift that is in thee, which was given thee by prophecy, with the laying on of the hands of the presbytery. Meditate upon these things; give thyself wholly to them; that thy profiting may appear to all. Take heed unto thyself, and unto the doctrine; continue in them: for in doing this thou shalt both save thyself, and them that hear thee.*

1Timothy 5:21-22 *I charge thee before God, and the Lord Jesus Christ, and the elect angels, that thou observe these things without preferring one before another, doing nothing by partiality. Lay hands suddenly on no man, neither be partaker of other men's sins: keep thyself pure. Drink no longer water, but use a little wine for thy stomach's sake and thine often infirmities.*

1Timothy 6:11-20 *But thou, O man of God, flee these things; and follow after righteousness, godliness, faith, love, patience, meekness. Fight the good fight of faith, lay hold on eternal life, whereunto thou art also called,* *and hast professed a good profession before many witnesses. I give thee charge in the sight of God, who quickeneth all things, and before Christ Jesus, who before Pontius Pilate witnessed a good confession; That thou keep this commandment without spot, unrebukeable, until the appearing of our Lord Jesus Christ: Which in his times he shall shew, who is the blessed and only Potentate, the King of kings, and Lord of lords; Who only hath immortality, dwelling in the light which no man can approach unto; whom no man hath seen, nor can see: to whom be honour and power everlasting. Amen.*

Charge them that are rich in this world, that they be not highminded, nor trust in uncertain riches, but in the living God, who giveth us richly all things to enjoy; That they do good, that they be rich in good works, ready to distribute, willing to communicate; Laying up in store for themselves a good foundation against the time to come, that they may lay hold on eternal life. O Timothy, keep that which is committed to thy trust, avoiding profane and vain babblings, and oppositions of science falsely so called: Which some professing have erred concerning the faith. Grace be with thee. Amen.

2Timothy 2:1-7 *Thou therefore, my son, be strong in the grace that is in Christ Jesus. And the things that thou hast heard of me among many witnesses, the same commit thou to faithful men, who shall be able to teach others also. Thou therefore endure hardness, as a good soldier of Jesus Christ. No man that warreth entangleth himself with the affairs of this life; that he may please him who hath chosen him to be a soldier. And if a man also strive for masteries, yet is he not crowned, except he strive lawfully. The husbandman that laboureth must be first partaker of the fruits. Consider what I say; and the Lord give thee understanding in all things.*

2Timothy 2:14-15 *Hold fast the form of sound words, which thou hast heard of me, in faith and love which is in Christ Jesus. That good thing which was committed unto thee keep by the Holy Ghost which dwelleth in us.*

2Timothy 3:10-12 *But thou hast fully known my doctrine, manner of life, purpose, faith, longsuffering, charity, patience, Persecutions, afflictions, which came unto me at Antioch, at Iconium, at Lystra; what persecutions I endured: but out of them all the Lord delivered me. Yea, and all that will live godly in Christ Jesus shall suffer persecution.*

2Timothy 4:1-5 *I charge thee therefore before God, and the Lord Jesus Christ, who shall judge the quick and the dead at his appearing and his kingdom; Preach the word; be instant in season, out of season; reprove, rebuke, exhort with all longsuffering and doctrine. For the time will come when they will not endure sound doctrine; but after their own lusts shall they heap to themselves teachers, having itching ears; And they shall turn away their ears from the truth, and shall be turned unto fables. But watch thou in all things, endure afflictions, do the work of an evangelist, make full proof of thy ministry.*

1Corinthians 4:17 *For this cause have I sent unto you Timotheus, who is my beloved son, and faithful in the Lord, who shall bring you into remembrance of my ways which be in Christ, as I teach every where in every church.*

Romans 16:21 *Timotheus my workfellow, and Lucius, and Jason, and Sosipater, my kinsmen, salute you.*

Philippians 2:19-22 *But I trust in the Lord Jesus to send Timotheus shortly unto you, that I also may be of good comfort, when I know your state. For I have no man likeminded, who will naturally care for your state. For all seek their own, not the things which are Jesus Christ's. But ye know the proof of him, that, as a son with the father, he hath served with me in the gospel.*

Elijah & Elisha
Elijah told Elisha that if he was around when the mantle dropped, it was his. Elisha walked with Elijah in ministry and was prepared and aligned as a successor. When the mantle dropped, he was right there to pick it up and proceed with performing double the miracles, signs, and wonders that Elijah did.

2Kings 2:9-13 *And it came to pass, when they were gone over, that Elijah said unto Elisha, Ask what I shall do for thee, before I be taken away from thee. And Elisha said, I pray thee, let a double portion of thy spirit be upon me. And he said, Thou hast asked a hard thing: nevertheless, if thou see me when I am taken from thee, it shall be so unto thee; but if not, it shall not be so. And it came to pass, as they still went on, and talked, that, behold, there appeared a chariot of fire, and horses of fire, and parted them both asunder; and Elijah went up by a whirlwind into heaven. And Elisha saw it, and he cried, My father, my father, the chariot of Israel, and the horsemen thereof. And he saw him no more: and he took hold of his own*

> *clothes, and rent them in two pieces. He took up also the mantle of Elijah that fell from him, and went back, and stood by the bank of Jordan.*

I believe one of the reasons people think that apostles and prophets were not for today is because many of the apostles were so focused on doing the work that they did not properly position successors. They raised up and discipled saints but not successors. They positioned people to assist with the work of the kingdom but not to carry the fullness of their legacy once they left the earth. In many ways, they failed to properly prepare the next generation to carry their legacy. So people took on the error that when they died, these offices and works of the spirit died with them. This is a grand misunderstanding that has no biblical truth. God is all about generational inheritance, successorship, and being known and glorified all down through the generations.

We want them to be mightier than us, carry the vision better, the gospel better, advance the kingdom better, and reap the harvest and blessings of God greater than we did

---

> ***Psalms 78:5-7*** *For He established a testimony (an express precept) in Jacob and appointed a law in Israel, commanding our fathers that they should make [the great facts of God's dealings with Israel] known to their children, that the generation to come might know them, that the children still to be born might arise and recount them to their children, that they might set their hope in God and not forget the works of God, but might keep His commandments.*

<u>Moses & The Israelites</u>
One of the greatest impartations Moses and the Israelites gave their younger generations was to prepare them for the Promised Land, and to SHIFT them into the inheritance that was due them.

> ***Joshua 1:1-9*** *Now after the death of Moses the servant of the Lord it came to pass, that the Lord spake unto Joshua the son of Nun, Moses' minister, saying, Moses my servant is dead; now therefore arise, go over this Jordan, thou, and all this people, unto the land which I do give to them, even to the children of Israel. Every place that the sole of your foot shall tread upon, that have I given unto you, as I said unto Moses. From the wilderness and this Lebanon even unto the great river, the river*

Euphrates, all the land of the Hittites, and unto the great sea toward the going down of the sun, shall be your coast. There shall not any man be able to stand before thee all the days of thy life: as I was with Moses, so I will be with thee: I will not fail thee, nor forsake thee. Be strong and of a good courage: for unto this people shalt thou divide for an inheritance the land, which I sware unto their fathers to give them. Only be thou strong and very courageous, that thou mayest observe to do according to all the law, which Moses my servant commanded thee: turn not from it to the right hand or to the left, that thou mayest prosper whithersoever thou goest. This book of the law shall not depart out of thy mouth; but thou shalt meditate therein day and night, that thou mayest observe to do according to all that is written therein: for then thou shalt make thy way prosperous, and then thou shalt have good success. Have not I commanded thee? Be strong and of a good courage; be not afraid, neither be thou dismayed: for the Lord thy God is with thee whithersoever thou goest.

Joshua 14:6-14 *Then the children of Judah came unto Joshua in Gilgal: and Caleb the son of Jephunneh the Kenezite said unto him, Thou knowest the thing that the Lord said unto Moses the man of God concerning me and thee in Kadeshbarnea. Forty years old was I when Moses the servant of the Lord sent me from Kadeshbarnea to espy out the land; and I brought him word again as it was in mine heart. Nevertheless my brethren that went up with me made the heart of the people melt: but I wholly followed the Lord my God. And Moses sware on that day, saying, Surely the land whereon thy feet have trodden shall be thine inheritance, and thy children's for ever, because thou hast wholly followed the LORD my God.*

And now, behold, the Lord hath kept me alive, as he said, these forty and five years, even since the Lord spake this word unto Moses, while the children of Israel wandered in the wilderness: and now, lo, I am this day fourscore and five years old. As yet I am as strong this day as I was in the day that Moses sent me: as my strength was then, even so is my strength now, for war, both to go out, and to come in. Now therefore give me this mountain, whereof the Lord spake in that day; for thou heardest in that day how the Anakims were there, and that the cities were great and fenced: if so be the Lord will be with me, then I shall be able to drive them out, as the Lord said. And Joshua blessed him, and gave unto Caleb the son of Jephunneh Hebron for an inheritance. Hebron therefore became the inheritance of Caleb the son of Jephunneh the Kenezite unto this day, because that he wholly followed the Lord God of Israel.

> ***Deuteronomy 11:24*** *Every place whereon the soles of your feet shall tread shall be yours: from the wilderness and Lebanon, from the river, the river Euphrates, even unto the uttermost sea shall your coast be.*

Had they not done this, all of what they achieved would have died in the wilderness. Even though Moses and the Israelites died, their seed lived and journeyed in places their feet never treaded. Their seed was able to achieve and advance the fullness of the promises that was given to them. This is key because there may be works that you will begin as the initial vision carrier, however, your seed will have to further plow and build that vision in order for the fullness of it to manifest in the earth.

A vital key we discern in examining godly biblical successors is that they are not clones. They possess the spiritual DNA of their leaders, but this does not make them clones.

Dictionary.com defines *DNA* as, "the fundamental and distinctive characteristics or qualities of someone or something, especially when regarded as unchangeable."

There may be undeniable and unchangeable distinct similarities regarding character, gifts, anointing wells, and ministry capabilities yet, successors have their own distinct identity that enhance their DNA and who they are to the leader. Their unique identity is essential to solidifying, empowering, and advancing what that leader carries.

Saul and David possessed Kingly DNA, yet, their unique identity distinguished them in their ability to be a godly king.

- Both possessed the qualities fit for a king (*1Samuel 8, 1Samuel 16*).
- Both were chosen kings - Saul was chosen by man (*1Samuel 8, 1Samuel 10:23-24*) and David was chosen by God (*1Samuel 16, 2Samuel 8:7-16*). David was then chosen by the people after Saul's death (*2Samuel 2*).
- Both were anointed as King by Prophet Samuel (*1Samuel 9, 1Samuel 16*).
- Both found favor in the eyes of the people (*1Samuel 9-10, 1Samuel 18:5, 15-16*) However, Saul desired the favor of the people over the favor of God (*1Samuel 18: 6-8*). David desired the favor and heart of God (*Psalms 119:34, Psalms 119:47-48, Acts 13:22*).

- Both started off with strong allegiance to God but then they both sinned. Saul sinned for self-gain and was unrepentant (*1Samuel 15:15*). David sinned, was repentant and after God's heart (*2Samuel 12:13, Psalms 25:11, Psalms 51*).
- Both were warriors and had songs written about their warfare accomplishments (*1Samuel 18:7-9*).

Saul failed to govern his DNA or to value David's DNA and unique identity. Though from a respected family and good upbringing, Saul's identity possessed character flaws and ungodly actions that caused him to be self-focused, people focused and disobedient to the directions of the Lord. This resulted in him being rejected by God. God's spirit departed from him and he often battled a tormenting demonic spirit that further challenged his effectiveness as king.

Though Saul needed David to experience healing, sanity, and to win difficult wars, he was jealous, conscientious, fearful of David, and dishonoring of the favor, blessings, and abilities of David. He thus became an enemy rather than a mentor, leader, or spiritual father to David.

> ***1Samuel 18:7-16*** *And the women answered one another as they played, and said, Saul hath slain his thousands, and David his ten thousands. And Saul was very wroth, and the saying displeased him; and he said, They have ascribed unto David ten thousands, and to me they have ascribed but thousands: and what can he have more but the kingdom? And Saul eyed David from that day and forward. And it came to pass on the morrow, that the evil spirit from God came upon Saul, and he prophesied in the midst of the house: and David played with his hand, as at other times: and there was a javelin in Saul's hand. And Saul cast the javelin; for he said, I will smite David even to the wall with it. And David avoided out of his presence twice.*
>
> *And Saul was afraid of David, because the Lord was with him, and was departed from Saul. Therefore Saul removed him from him, and made him his captain over a thousand; and he went out and came in before the people. And David behaved himself wisely in all his ways; and the Lord was with him. Wherefore when Saul saw that he behaved himself very wisely, he was afraid of him. But all Israel and Judah loved David, because he went out and came in before them.*

Saul was jealous rather than celebrating of the enhancement of a successor that David was to him. He only wanted to kill David for the unique identity he had and spent much of his destiny trying to murder what should have enhanced and advanced his throne and kingdom. This is the result when we view successors as threats rather than blessings.

David had a heart for Saul but Saul did not have a heart for David. Saul initially loved David, but then hated him when he recognized they had similar DNA.

> *1Samuel 16:21-23 And David came to Saul, and stood before him: and he loved him greatly; and he became his armourbearer. And Saul sent to Jesse, saying, Let David, I pray thee, stand before me; for he hath found favour in my sight. And it came to pass, when the evil spirit from God was upon Saul, that David took an harp, and played with his hand: so Saul was refreshed, and was well, and the evil spirit departed from him.*

Saul loved David when he was more of a servant. This SHIFTED when Saul realized David could be his equal or even greater than him. This happens all too often in the body of Christ among leaders and potential successors. The very things the leader initially loves SHIFTS to hatred when they realize the potential successor is not called to be beneath them, but beside them, and even are to replace and advance them.

David's heart was so for Saul that he refused to touch his anointing even though Saul's actions warranted rebuke, correction and even death.

> *Psalms 105:13-15 When they went from one nation to another, from one kingdom to another people; He suffered no man to do them wrong: yea, he reproved kings for their sakes; Saying, Touch not mine anointed, and do my prophets no harm.*

David never tried to usurp Saul even though he was anointed to be king, could have justifiably killed Saul and taken the throne. David remained in the roles that was given to him by Saul, even though many of these positions were to keep David from the throne. David soared in these positions which gave him more favor and honor with the people. David did not allow this regard to incite pride where he would consider usurping. This demonstrates the character of a true successor. They are not seeking to take the position of their leader or successorship before

God's timing. They are not willing to sacrifice the spiritual and natural life of their leader for fame, fortune, success or personal advancement.

David had such a godly heart for Saul until he grieved Saul's death as if they had actually journeyed together in covenant successorship.

> ***2Samuel 1:13-21*** *And David said unto the young man that told him, Whence art thou? And he answered, I am the son of a stranger, an Amalekite. And David said unto him, How wast thou not afraid to stretch forth thine hand to destroy the Lord's anointed? And David called one of the young men, and said, Go near, and fall upon him. And he smote him that he died. And David said unto him, Thy blood be upon thy head; for thy mouth hath testified against thee, saying, I have slain the Lord's anointed.*
>
> *And David lamented with this lamentation over Saul and over Jonathan his son: (Also he bade them teach the children of Judah the use of the bow: behold, it is written in the book of Jasher.) The beauty of Israel is slain upon thy high places: how are the mighty fallen! Tell it not in Gath, publish it not in the streets of Askelon; lest the daughters of the Philistines rejoice, lest the daughters of the uncircumcised triumph. Ye mountains of Gilboa, let there be no dew, neither let there be rain, upon you, nor fields of offerings: for there the shield of the mighty is vilely cast away, the shield of Saul, as though he had not been anointed with oil.*

There are some successors out there who are grieving the lives of their leaders or grieving the lack of covenant they should be having with them. MY GOD! Decreeing healing right now in Jesus name.

Successors have the heart of God for those they are called to. God's heart for their leader is engrained within them and despite what occurs, they will find it difficult to hurt, revenge, betray, usurp, dishonor, leave, or expose that leader. If others touch the leader, the successor will invoke judgment and justice, while seeking a way to restore honor upon the leader. Successors leave it to God to judge their leader, while they uphold their duty as successors. Many see this as false loyalty by covering the sins of a fallen leader. But the successor views it as their duty as one who carries the heart and legacy of God for that leader.

Successors should be sought after, groomed in the character and nature of God, trained to carry the vision, and positioned in their role of successorship. They should not be punished, stifled, or hazed as they did not choose this position. It was ordained by God. He chooses the successor. Johnathan, Saul's son who should have inherited the throne, understood this revelation. He did not despise David for being chosen. He loved David as his own soul and assisted him in any way he could in being prepared and aligned in his successorship.

> *1Samuel 18:1-4 And it came to pass, when he had made an end of speaking unto Saul, that the soul of Jonathan was knit with the soul of David, and Jonathan loved him as his own soul. And Saul took him that day, and would let him go no more home to his father's house. Then Jonathan and David made a covenant, because he loved him as his own soul. And Jonathan stripped himself of the robe that was upon him, and gave it to David, and his garments, even to his sword, and to his bow, and to his girdle.*
>
> (***Also Study 1Samuel 20-22***)

A successor should receive hands on training as they walk along side of leaders in carrying and releasing the vision. They are learning the heart, character, nature and standards necessary for embodying and governing the vision. They are learning God's will and purpose for the vision and how to bring it to pass in the earth.

Successors will make mistakes, will sometimes require correction or rebuke, will assert their independence in unfavorable times, as after all they do have their own unique identity in addition to successorship. These are teachable moments to groom them into the character, nature, and standards of God. These are not moments to strip them of their successorship, control them, or make them feel like they have to walk on eggshells to prove they are capable of carrying the leader's legacy. In these instances, many leaders place stipulations and even spoken and unspoken rules upon the successor where they feel they can lose their legacy at any time. But the legacy is never to be bargained with. It is not really necessary to do this because the successor's journey in and of itself will draw them to or terminate them from being a successor. The vision itself is designed to expose the ungodly. All these erred mindsets of stripping someone and beating them down before building them up and utilizing them is not of God. All these mindsets of people having to walk in ones shoes before they can have what they have or do what they do is unbiblical. As fivefold leaders, we pave the way and plow terrain so that others can build upon it, not relive it. We have a heart for the future generations. We want them to be mightier than us, carry the vision better, the gospel better, advance the kingdom better, and reap the harvest and blessings of God greater than we did. This is the heart and character of a true leader and is the fruit we should be experiencing as we pour into our successors and saints alike.

I have multiple successors in my ministry. My main successor is being groomed to lead the ministry, to distribute the ministry to the other successors, and to govern it properly where it can continue to live and advance throughout generations until Jesus comes. She is being taught to lead, equip and empower all those who are a part of the ministry and to journey in covenant with the other successors. They are learning to trust and honor her as a major leader and how they are to carry the vision together as a team to advance the ministry from generation to generation. My main successor is a go getter. She is bold, confident, fierce, fiery, teachable, repent quickly, loving, feisty, kind and headstrong. She has the heart of God for me, the vision, the team and the members. She has already exceeded me in many ways. I am not requiring her to be me or to be perfect. I give her opportunities to grow and to be utilized in her personal identity and successorship and God gives us revelation of how to journey together as she learns how to be the future vision carrier of the ministry. This gives me the ability to work and expand other areas of the vision while continuing to flourish in the portions that have already been established. Leaders do not be afraid to release your successors. Pour your life into them and give them ample opportunity to carry your vision all down through the generations. SHIFT!

Homework Explorations:
1. Journal on at least three stories from this chapter and discuss what you learned regarding their successorship.
2. If someone was to carry your spiritual DNA what would their characteristics be?
3. List five important reasons successorship is necessary?
4. Journal regarding your destiny and calling and what you hope to leave to the next generation.
5. Journal how your fivefold ministry impacts the generations now and generations to come.
6. Journal five goals you can implement to prepare your successors to carry your DNA to the next generation.

DEMONIC HOOKS THAT KEEP YOU IN THE OLD

As you strive to SHIFT from the old paradigm into fivefold paradigm, certain spirits, cycles, and psychological attacks will come for you. They want to SHIFT you back and keep you tied to the old.

Psychological Warfare (Study the story of Nehemiah) - Derives from territorial spirits, powers, spells and word curses, and witchcraft sent from witches, warlocks, and demonic chatter from demons, ungodly, foolish or ignorant people. Words live on airways and demons pick them up, especially the negative ones. Then they speak them back to you to distract, weary and kill your progress or stance in God. This warfare causes anxiety, insecurity, and a wrestling and questioning of God's word.

Break the powers of wrestling and questioning. Boldly muzzle and silence demonic voices by telling them to SHUT UP! Break the powers of spells, sooth saying, psychic powers and telepathy being sent against you. Use the blood of Jesus to cleanse airways and frequencies of ungodly, negative, and demonic words that have been spoken about you.

Mental Warfare - can come from the insecurities of your soul - your inner man, or from the principalities and powers and frequencies and airways within your midst. It entails a continuous flood of vile thoughts, misperceptions, mental oppression, fear and doubt, confusion, forgetfulness, migraines, demonic suggestions and impressions. The voices of your soul, or of the enemy are strong and speaking continually to weaken your mind, your stance and your ability to journey in the truths, purposes, strategies, visions, and momentum of the Lord. You may feel crazy and like you are losing your mind, focus, faith, and stability.

It is important to deal with the wounded and insecure issues of your soul as this will help silence mental warfare. Also muzzle the mouths and airways of demonic forces around you while cleansing mental instability and pressuring words that have been released concerning you within the frequencies and airways of your region.

Emotional Warfare - Attacks your emotions and senses while causing double mindedness, confusion, frustration, pressure, depression and oppression. Makes you feel dramatic and out of control like you are on an emotional rollercoaster. Can cause you to appear manic, bipolar, or schizophrenic. Can operate through condemnation and uses shame and guilt of being unstable to further draw you away and isolate you from your supports and accountability partners. Causes weeping, uncontrollable crying for no apparent reason or regarding things that would not warrant crying. Evokes thoughts of suicide, death and failure thoughts. Attacks your body's hormonal system to further confound emotional instability and affliction (e.g., PMS, thyroid issues, digestive issues, blood pressure issues, migraines, anxiety, panic, nervousness, body aches and pains).

Insecurity, immaturity, unworthiness, and/or comparison, fear of the unknown, fear of failing, life stressors, burnout, can open the doors to this attack. Bewitchment from people, witches, and demons can also cause this attack.

You must be discerning that this attack will occur or you will give fully into it. You will spend days distracted, losing time, focus and momentum due to succumbing to it. It will in turn, take time to SHIFT out of it due to its impact. It will feel like you are SHIFTING up out of a pit or dark place.

Receiving prayer and encouragement immediately is key to nullifying this attack. Come up out of this attack by reconnecting with supports, receiving prayer, fellowship, and truth. Spend time soaking in the love of God; spend time rehearsing and decreeing out promises, and prophecies of God.

Financial Warfare - Will come as the spirit of Python to squeeze out the vision finances and cause financial hardship. Come to make you believe you cannot fund the vision; it is too big and cannot be financed. Will cause psychological warfare of worry regarding money. Apostle Jackie Green, founder of The Enternational Prayerlife Institute, says this spirit will *"cause attacks in areas of job security, bank accounts, old bills arise from the past, garnishment of wages, stress on the church finances and unexpected expenses eat away at monies. Enemy will attack your faithful tithers and givers to cause them to leave the church or be attacked in their income so they cannot give."*

Consistently contend against the spirit of Python. Continuously release the vision to God and declare miracles and prosperity blessings to manifest on your behalf. Take on the mindset that the vision is God's so he will find it, and expect him to do just that. Share your concerns and fears with God concerning finances and allow him to build and encourage your faith as needed. Ask God for witty ideas for creating multiple streams of income. Command prophetic words and promises concerning finances and prosperity to manifest in your life. Decree out wealth transfers from the wicked and for favor with people to sow consistently into your life and vision. Decree into the glory and SHIFT heaven to earth on your behalf. Deal with any brass heavens, poverty spirits, and personal and generational strongholds that may be hindering the flow of favor, mercy, grace, and prosperity.

> ***Proverbs 8:12*** *I wisdom dwell with prudence, and find out knowledge of witty inventions.*
>
> ***Psalms 104:24*** *O LORD, how manifold are thy works! in wisdom hast thou made them all: the earth is full of thy riches.*
>
> ***Philippians 4:19*** *But my God shall supply all your need according to his riches in glory by Christ Jesus.*
>
> ***Proverbs 13:22*** *A good man leaveth an inheritance to his children's children: and the wealth of the sinner is laid up for the just.*

Python Spirits- Spirits that come to slowly squeeze the life out of the vision carriers, members, and the vision. This spirit comes as depression, heaviness, financial hardship, subtle drainage of an area/s of your life and vision. It will wrap around a person, family, situation, and ministry, or region, vision, while using its body to squeeze and restrict them where:

- They are limited in mobility and progress
- There may also be an unexplainable tiredness and lethargic oppression where energy, movement, and progress is slow or thwarted
- There will be a weightiness, physical suffocation, over exertion in energy, and sluggardness to being in step with the momentum of God

- It causes confusion, discombobulation, double mindedness, and thought racing, from the signal faculties in the brain being restricted, weighty and crushed

Python comes to squeeze the life out of people, families, churches, ministries, relationships, and the region spiritually, physically, financially, economically, mentally and emotionally, etc. Comes against new ministries and businesses with a vengeance to thwart and abort the vision and hinder them from planting and developing. Seeks to kill them early by causing constriction and suffocation. This is done through suffocation and constriction. Death is generally slow and painful. The snake:

- Sits on the person's shoulders and makes them sluggish and lethargic
- Will wrap around a person, ministry or region to attempt to constrict to squeeze out the life, production, zeal, fruit and success of that person, ministry or region
- Will wrap around the head revelation and vision and cause headaches and pressure

Also works through:

- Divination/Soothsaying (Gothic, astrology, and Baal)
- Pharmakia (hallucinate drugs; street drugs, prescribed pain pills, psychiatric drugs)
- Apathy – makes a person, atmosphere or region lethargic, sluggish, indifferent, passive, cold, lacking of drive for life
- Depression – especially strong in the fall leading to the winter months. Winters tend to be very long, the cold weather is bitter and hard, which makes life secluded and difficult
- Heaviness (constant feeling of a weighing down)
- Word curses, witchcraft
- Fear – sluggardness and indifferent feelings sensations causing anxiety, fear, fear of dying, fear of failing
- Discouragement - hopelessness that tends to hit a person or atmosphere when there are not any challenging situations going on or heightens when situations may be occurring
- Infirmity – will cause sicknesses that comes in the form of feeling pressured or weighed down. Can also cause

respiratory illnesses or sensations like inability to breathe or choking

Isaiah 61:3 To appoint unto them that mourn in Zion, to give unto them beauty for ashes, the oil of joy for mourning, the garment of praise for the spirit of heaviness; that they might be called trees of righteousness, the planting of the Lord, that he might be glorified.

Break the head and tail of the python. Loose Holy fire to torment it where it releases its grip, while commanding this spirit to uncoil and be cast out of your midst. Continuously decree, promote, and release life and that more abundantly as death cannot flourish where God's light and resurrection life dwells.

Spirits of Fear - These spirits will come in the form of spiritual warfare. They will constantly try to make you feel insecure, inept, and inferior of the SHIFT you are embarking upon. They will be attempting to break you down - weary you - until you give up altogether or return to what is comfortable and familiar.

- Fear of failing
- Fear of looking ill equipped
- Fear of engaging in false and erred doctrine
- Fear of making the wrong decisions and moves
- Fear of leading people wrong
- Fear of losing control and order of people and the ministry
- Fear of losing what has already been built
- Fear of losing members
- Fear of being alone - losing friends, loved ones, ministry partners who do not understand or believe in fivefold
- Fear of losing destiny and ministry momentum
- Fear of being ridiculed and judged
- Fear of the warfare of SHIFTING into a new paradigm or that accompanies fivefold ministry
- Fear of not having avenues to be trained and equipped
- Fear of not being ready for fivefold ministry and all it entails

Stand on the word against these spirits:

>*2Timothy 1:7* For God hath not given us the spirit of fear; but of power, and of love, and of a sound mind. SHIFT!
>
>*1John 4:4* You are of God, little children, and have overcome them, because He who is in you is greater than he who is in the world.
>
>*Philippians 4:13* I can do all things through Christ who strengthens me.
>
>*John 10:27* My sheep hear my voice, and I know them, and they follow me:
>
>*Isaiah 11:2* The Spirit of the LORD will rest on Him--the Spirit of wisdom and understanding, the Spirit of counsel and strength, the Spirit of knowledge and the fear of the LORD.
>
>*John 14:27* Peace I leave with you; My peace I give to you. I do not give to you as the world gives. Do not let your hearts be troubled; do not be afraid.
>
>*Romans 8:15* For you did not receive a spirit of slavery that returns you to fear, but you received the Spirit of sonship, by whom we cry, "Abba! Father!"
>
>*Romans 8:31* What then shall we say to these things? If God is for us, who can be against us?
>
>*Isaiah 54:15-17* Indeed they shall surely assemble, but not because of Me. Whoever assembles against you shall fall for your sake. "Behold, I have created the blacksmith Who blows the coals in the fire, Who brings forth an instrument for his work; And I have created the spoiler to destroy. No weapon formed against you shall prosper, And every tongue which rises against you in judgment You shall condemn. This is the heritage of the servants of the Lord, And their righteousness is from Me," Says the Lord.
>
>*2Corinthians 2:14* Now thanks be to God who always leads us in triumph in Christ, and through us diffuses the fragrance of His knowledge in every place.

Destiny Killing Spirit - Attacks personally and generationally. It wants to kill your destiny, and any way God's plan for your life impacts your success, advancement, lineage, and present and future generations.

> *John 10:10* *The thief cometh not, but for to steal, and to kill, and to destroy: I am come that they might have life, and that they might have it more abundantly.*

This spirit usually begins its attack at a young age, even at birth, and then attempts to kill the person's identity, purpose, and hope at a young age. This is the reason so many believers, especially leaders, experience challenging childhoods. The enemy is striving to kill the person before they realize there is a plan for their lives. This spirit knows that if you align with true fivefold, destiny is inevitable.

It will do everything possible to murder or get you to murder, altar or stifle the vision and plan God is providing for your life. It will blatantly try to kill you, send people to try to kill you spiritually and naturally through words, enticements, seductions; come through sickness and affliction, try to steal and kill the seeds you plant, release constant warfare to get you to quit, present favorable or easier altering paths so you compromise. You have to want what God has for you more than what the devil or man can offer. You have to get to a place of being souled out and wanting to please God at all cost.

Identify personal and generational destiny killing spirits, how they come for you, when they come for you, and how they manifest in people and in situations around you. Break their powers over your life and generational line. Cancel their assignments against your life and generations. Close up doors in and around you that allow them to enter your sphere of influence. Break and resist cycles and behavioral patterns of sabotage, disobedience, rebellion, and anti-submissiveness as this opens the door to the operation of destiny killing spirits.

Backsliding Spirit - This spirit will cause you to relapse into old familiar habits, religious and traditional behavior and activities. This spirit will make you believe that what you had was better than where God is taking you. It will have all types of excuses as to the reason you should stay or return to the old. It will point out all your flaws, the challenges of moving forward, make you feel obligated to the old, and responsible for others not being able to fill your position. It will cause you to endure psychological and mental warfare that makes you feel insecure and the unknown and the future. It will present the old as productive, fruitful, beneficial, and prosperous. And even if these attributes hold truth, if it is not where God wants you then you are in sin due to disobedience and are reaping from an illegal place of familiarity. Such harvest often comes with consequences where you eventually insure drama and calamity from the place or people to which you are reaping or receive the judgment of the Lord due to being disobedient.

Spend time repenting for backsliding ways, cycles, sin issues, and disobedience towards the purposes of God. Break the powers of rebellion and anti-submissiveness and break all soul ties with the old (e.g the people, ministry, positions, duties, etc.). Spend time closing doors to the old and decreeing out new doors, visions and purposes. Spend time seeking God for clarity, vision, and love for the new SHIFTED vision he is bringing you into. Seek accountability partners that can help you remain grounded in the new vision. Be obedient to what God is saying while fasting weekly to kill your flesh and subject your soul to your spirit where you can walk confidently in the will and purposes of God.

Spirit Of The Crab - This spirit moves sideways and never forward, and attempts to get you to do this as well. It will try to sidetrack you, delay, and sideline you from the purposes of God. It will try to get you to feel that you are not ready and will present all types of excuses as the reason you should wait, should not go forward, and the reasons you are not equipped to do what God has already told and trained you to do. When natural crabs are clumped together, they will pull one another down in order to get ahead or out of a sticky spot. This spirit operates in the same manner. It tries to pull you down or off the correct path with God especially when you are gaining some progress and momentum in God. It attempts to pull you to a place of sidetracking, backsliding, and regression. It will attempt to stifle your success and advancement where you are working on the same thing over and over again, while never progressing or moving past a certain point in your life.

This spirit will also try to keep you soul tied to the old by providing opportunities that appear to be favorable, profitable, and for the betterment of all parties when really it is just to keep you attached to the old and distracted in advancing where God is taking you. Break this spirits legs as it uses its claws of words, belittlement, error, obligation, false loyalty, plan B, seduction, manipulation, intimidation, pride, sin, poverty and low level mindsets and behaviors, etc., to snatch you back down to its downgraded level or a level beneath God's will for your life. This spirit will be seeking to own and use you but you will not be aware of it because of the flattery and seduction to which it presents.

Spirits of Religion & Tradition aka Ungodly Vision Dictators - People will come and want you to be and implement a traditional paradigm when God has given you a unique fivefold blueprint. They are going to want Sunday services, bible studies, Sunday school, men's ministries, women's ministries, and so on. They will not have vision for your blueprint but will see the potential of the old inside the physical space God has given you. They will speak against your vision, question it, and tell you how unrealistic and far-fetched it is. They will sow seeds of fear as it relates to your ability to succeed, fund the vision, or draw people to the vision. They will tell you how great and safe the religious and traditional paradigm is and make you feel it is best for you and those God has called you to.

Do not allow people to dictate, implement their familiarity on you or place a vision on you that God did not give you. If they cannot align with the vision God sets, then they are not your remnant and that is okay. There is a ministry, business, etc., for them. Encourage them to connect to them, while remaining true to the blueprint God has called you to. You will know your remnant. Your remnant will value the vision and want to align to it. They will want who you are and what God has called you to do in the earth. If they want an altered vision implemented then they need to run with it by planting it themselves - not you.

Do not allow it to sow seeds of negativity, discord, fear, and witchcraft curses into you or your ministry. Have a clear understanding of your identity, purpose and vision so you can immediately shut down this spirit when it manifests. Be okay with silencing this spirit with the truth of the vision and rebuke and correct it and anyone else that agrees with it. Do not give these people major roles in your ministry until they show clear signs of being delivered from this spirit. Otherwise, they will sow tares and wreak havoc in your ministry and the unity of your team. They will seek to get people on their side as they release subtle word curses to discredit you and the vision and to draw people back into familiar paradigms that appear more logical and easier to implement. Value quality over quantity and know that few in number is better than having people on the team that do not have your heart for the vision.

Legalism - Is the act of putting ungodly laws or the laws of the land above the gospel of Jesus Christ, above the laws and standards of God, or above what God is purposing concerning your life or situation. These laws can be laws of your community, state, nation; laws on your job, laws of an organization, policies and procedures, legal requirements; school rules or requirements, culture trends, traditions of man, your family; laws and doctrines of ministries and businesses, that are used by the enemy to stifle what God has purposed, is planting, building, etc. Or that wants you to disobey the laws and standards of God's word.

You have to trust God to prevail for you. It will initially appear as you will not win. Do not waver or fear. But stand decreeing and contending for the judgment, justice, and purpose of God to manifest, as he will prevail for you.

False or Immature Place Holders - Be okay with people gleaning but not being your remnant. There will be seasonal people, inconsistent followers, church hoppers, and sojourners. Per Apostle Oscar Guobadia, Founder of the Brook Place Ministries in United Kingdom London, sojourners are those you instruct and impart into but are not your remnant). You will always have people like this show up at your ministry and that is okay. They can be a blessing to you in certain ways as they glean and connect with you and your ministry and you and your ministry can be a blessing to them. Accept what they can give, do not take it personal when they do not support and invest sufficiently; and do not see it as dishonor when they are not committed to your vision. They are not supposed to be committed because they are not your remnant. Yet, they may be just as important to awakening revival reformation in the region as you are as they may be connected to someone else's ministry or sent to be temporary assistant. Or they may be sent to give what they can but nothing more. Receive them for where they are and do not give them complete access to the vision. Do not give them positions that they are not capable of filling. If they want more access to the vision then give them goals where they can mature into vision carriers. They will either mature where you can effectively utilize them or they will leave. Either way you are operating responsibly with protecting yourself and the vision.

Homework Explorations:

1. Journal in detail ways you have encountered these spirits and what you have learned from this chapter in how to combat them.
2. Journal how you would discern these spirits attack against your destiny and life's vision, and against the fivefold ministry vision you are helping to plant in the earth.
3. Write a decree to combat the attacks of these spirits against your destiny and life's vision.

WARFARE & SUFFERINGS AS A VISION CARRIER

Some of the information in this chapter is From Dr. Taquetta Baker's book *"Healing The Wounded Leader."*

> ***2Corinthians 10:3-****4 For though we walk in the flesh, we do not war after the flesh: (For the weapons of our warfare are not carnal , but mighty through God to the pulling down of strong holds).*

<u>Warfare</u> is <u>strateia</u> in Greek and means:
1. military service, i.e. (figuratively) the apostolic career (as one of hardship and danger): — warfare.
2. an expedition, campaign, military service, warfare
3. metaph. Paul likens his contest with the difficulties that oppose him in the discharge of his apostolic duties, as warfare

As leaders, fivefold ministers, vision carriers and saints of Jesus Christ, warfare is a part of our destiny and calling. And depending on the type of leader you are and the position you hold, the warfare is a career of warfare and danger. Apostle Paul likened his calling to being in military service. He used himself as an apostle to express that for some leaders, it is part of ones' calling to be opposed and to contend for the gospel of Jesus Christ. Therefore, the warfare should not be a shock or a challenge to you. It should be expected and embraced as a part of your calling.

This is so important because often we equate warfare as:

- ❖ Being out of the will of God or in sin.
- ❖ Not having enough faith or maturity concerning the things of God.
- ❖ Being in demonic oppression or bondage.
- ❖ An indicator that we are not successful or we are failing in our destiny or ministry.
- ❖ Or we do not adequately discern when warfare is not about our destiny and calling such that we are not aware of open doors in our lives and ministries.

Some believers contend that grace, not acknowledging, or focusing on the devil guards them from warfare. I have not found this to be biblical or reality. Our entire walk is rooted in asserting our authority over the enemy. Acting like the devil does not exist is not going to make him go away. He is coming for you whether you like it or not or whether you want to fight or not.

> ***Matthew 11:12*** *And from the days of John the Baptist until now the kingdom of heaven suffereth violence, and the violent take it by force.*

There has to be a balance in understanding that warfare is a part of our lifestyle as believers and especially as fivefold leaders and officers, and the importance of closing doors to unnecessary warfare. Since we know warfare is inevitable, we must engage it from an offensive position. Often, we are trying to defend ourselves from the warfare rather than being offensive in training ourselves as skilled warriors that attack the enemy before he attacks us; or close doors and gateways to attacks. In becoming offensive, we are asserting our authority and power over the enemy and our kingly right as believers and leading governmental officials in the earth. When we are offensive, we achieve and receive the victory that Jesus gave us through the works of the cross. We are asserting our authority over blessings and successes that rightfully belong to us. When we are defensive, it is like trying to perform Jesus' works all over again. We are trying to win something that is already ours. Instead of exercising our authority over what has already been won for us.

> ***1John 5:4*** *For whatever is born of God overcomes the world; and this is the victory that has overcome the world-- our faith.*

We do not have to be afraid of warfare because:

- God is a God of war (***Exodus 15:3***)
- God teaches us how to war (***Psalms 18:44, Psalms 144***)
- God gives us insight into the enemy's camp and how to defeat the enemy (***2Timothy 2:7, Daniel 9:22, 1Corinthians 2:12, Matthew 16:18-19***)
- We are already victorious (***Romans 8:37***)
- God provides insight concerning our calling and the warfare it entails (***Ephesians 1:18-19***)
- We have power over all the power of the enemy (***Luke 9:1, Luke 10:19***)
- The battles is not really ours, we are just vessels God uses; the battle is the Lords (***2Chronicles 20:25, Isaiah 54:17***)

As vision carriers and believers of fivefold ministries and offices, we must understand that our very position and the vision itself will invoke warfare. Anyone in a military office has an opposing enemy. Moreover, the more the fivefold vision is established and advanced, it will contend against the principalities and powers that are impacting the people, land, atmosphere, communities, regions and spheres. There is no way around this fact. Being offensive is even more important since knowing your enemy is essential being successful in establishing, building, and advancing the fivefold ministry vision. I am going to discuss this more in detail in a volume three, but want to note that personally and as a ministry, we should be seeking God for insight on the movements and activities of the enemy, and pursuing strategy on how to stop and defeat him.

> ***Psalms 44:5*** *Through You we will push down our enemies; through Your name we will trample those who rise up against us. For I will not trust in my bow, nor shall my sword save me. But You have saved us from our enemies, and have put to shame those who hated us. In God we boast all day long, and praise Your name forever.*

The devil should dread coming to our address because he knows we will be waiting on him and even attacking him before he gets there. I decree that as believers, vision carriers, fivefold leaders and officers you are SHIFTING from viewing warfare as part of your identity. SHIFT!

Homework Questions
1. Journal in detail what you learned about warfare from this chapter.
2. Journal how you have viewed warfare in the past and where your mindset and life's posture need to SHIFT regarding warfare.
3. Study and journal five warfare scriptures you need to stand on as it relates to your destiny and call.
4. Study the scriptures listed in this chapter regarding not being afraid of warfare. Journal what you learned.

DRINKING THE FULL CUP OF DESTINY

Many believers have a challenging time understanding the weight of the call and/or office as they are SHIFTING into their seat. The apostles did not really grasp the weight of their office until after the resurrection of Jesus Christ. They had titles, glory, signs, wonders, hands on training with Jesus, and positioning, but had not drank the full cup of destiny. Therefore, they were naive to the fullness of all their calling entailed.

> *Mark 10:35-40 The Message Bible* James and John, Zebedee's sons, came up to him. "Teacher, we have something we want you to do for us." "What is it? I'll see what I can do." "Arrange it," they said, "so that we will be awarded the highest places of honor in your glory – one of us at your right, the other at your left." Jesus said, "You have no idea what you're asking. Are you capable of drinking the cup I drink, of being baptized in the baptism I'm about to be plunged into?" "Sure," they said. "Why not?" Jesus said, "Come to think of it, you will drink the cup I drink, and be baptized in my baptism. But as to awarding places of honor, that's not my business. There are other arrangements for that."

> *The Amplified Bible Verse 38-39* But Jesus said to them, You do not know what you are asking. Are you able to drink the cup that I drink or be baptized with the baptism [of affliction] with which I am baptized? And they replied to Him, We are able. And Jesus told them, The cup that I drink you will drink, and you will be baptized with the baptism with which I am baptized.

Baptism of affliction????

<u>Cup</u> is *potērion* in Greek and means:
1. Cupful, lot of fate, a cup, a drinking vessel
2. metaph. one's lot or experience, whether joyous or adverse, divine appointments, whether favourable or unfavourable, are likened to a cup which God presents one to drink: so of prosperity and adversity

James, John and Zebedee's sons had been walking with Jesus for a time, so they were going to drink the cup of destiny whether they wanted to or not. Especially since Jesus was about to be crucified. There was a cup of destiny that was about to unfold by association with Jesus that they were not even cognizant of. And as they embodied that cup, they would also embody what Jesus was about to endure. As they experienced this

SHIFT, they would have to make decisions about destiny that would feel like they were being baptized in affliction as that was what the crucifixion felt like for Jesus. They loved the glam of ministry which is the reason they wanted the honor of sitting on the right and left side of Jesus, but they were naive to the cup of destiny that was about to be handed to them.

There are indeed awards of honor that come with drinking the cup, but obtaining this is based on motives and heart postures. This is the reason Jesus said he had nothing to do with the rewards they received. Their current posture was prideful, embodied competition and envy, and was for self-glory. As long as they remained in this state, the awards would be impure, fleeting and most likely would not align them with the kingdom rewards that would be due them.

> *This is a place where God has chosen you and has decided that your life is his.*

Also, once people realize they have to drink the cup, they may decide they do not want destiny or only want a measure of destiny. This too can impact the awards of honor that comes with drinking the cup.
I remember a season of dreading the cup I was drinking. I could not believe all I was enduring. Then God revealed to me how Jesus drank his cup of destiny in the garden of Gethsemane.

> *Matthew 26:36-46 Then cometh Jesus with them unto a place called Gethsemane, and saith unto the disciples, Sit ye here, while I go and pray yonder. And he took with him Peter and the two sons of Zebedee, and began to be sorrowful and very heavy. Then saith he unto them, My soul is exceeding sorrowful, even unto death: tarry ye here, and watch with me. And he went a little further, and fell on his face, and prayed, saying, O my Father, if it be possible, let this cup pass from me: nevertheless not as I will, but as thou wilt. And he cometh unto the disciples, and findeth them asleep, and saith unto Peter, What, could ye not watch with me one hour? Watch and pray, that ye enter not into temptation: the spirit indeed is willing, but the flesh is weak.*
>
> *He went away again the second time, and prayed, saying, O my Father, if this cup may not pass away from me, except I drink it, thy will be done.*

And he came and found them asleep again: for their eyes were heavy. And he left them, and went away again, and prayed the third time, saying the same words. Then cometh he to his disciples, and saith unto them, Sleep on now, and take your rest: behold, the hour is at hand, and the Son of man is betrayed into the hands of sinners. Rise, let us be going: behold, he is at hand that doth betray me.

Luke 22:41-46 *And he was withdrawn from them about a stone's cast, and kneeled down, and prayed, Saying, Father, if thou be willing, remove this cup from me: nevertheless not my will, but thine, be done. And there appeared an angel unto him from heaven, strengthening him. And being in an agony he prayed more earnestly: and his sweat was as it were great drops of blood falling down to the ground. And when he rose up from prayer, and was come to his disciples, he found them sleeping for sorrow, And said unto them, Why sleep ye? rise and pray, lest ye enter into temptation.*

Jesus said his soul was sorrowful and very heavy even unto death. This was an unexplainable anguish that Jesus was initially asking if it was possible to be released from. Jesus felt he needed prayer and support but his covenants had willing spirits but were weak in their flesh. Though they were physically present, they could not spiritually pray this cup of destiny away. Even with being strengthened in the presence of God and angels, the release of the dread that came with the cup ended only by drinking the full cup. Jesus had to endure persecution, crucifixion, death and the resurrection before he SHIFTED into drinking and becoming the full cup of destiny.

You will experience psychological and mental warfare as you endeavor to drink the cup.

- ❖ It will feel like you are dying at times. YOU ARE! You are spiritually dying to self, while coming to life in the fullness of your destiny with Jesus Christ and the utter spiritual stance of an officer.
- ❖ You will feel like running.
- ❖ You will feel like quitting.
- ❖ You will feel like you do not measure up.
- ❖ You will have a fear of failing and therefore will not want to try.
- ❖ You will feel discombobulated and emotionally unstable - double minded at times.

- You will feel like you are giving everything up for the call. YOU ARE! It will feel painful and grieving at times.
- You will be sold out one day and unsure the next.
- You will be appalled and grieved during times you recognize that you are not sold out. Will experience some shame and guilt because you are not where you thought you were and want to be.
- There will be an immediate conviction when you compromise and even feel like compromising. You will feel like you betraying God even with subtle sins because the weight of the call will yearn for purity, righteousness, holiness, virtue.
- You will make excuses for the reason you are not ready for the SHIFT of drinking the whole cup.
- You will have challenges SHIFTING from making heart decisions to governmental decisions that are clearly/purely about God's kingdom standards and principles.
- You will feel like you cannot handle the warfare that comes with the call. Much of the warfare is about what you have to give up which is internal, but it will all feel like it is external because of the constant psychological and mental dialog you are having with yourself, your inner man is having with your spirit man, and you are having with the devil.
- If you are a kingdom heir where you are restoring the blessings and kingdom of Jesus Christ back into your bloodline, then this may confound matters a bit. You will be contending against familiar spirits, generational curses, and contending for holiness within your bloodline. You may lose some family members for a season because of having to stand against ungodly systems, paradigms, and culture standards and loyalties in your line that do not align with the word and standard of God. You will have a challenge choosing God versus wanting to choose family members for the sake of avoiding conflict and not wanting to lose or cause tension in relationships.
- If you are a pioneer, entrepreneur, fivefold officer, and/or vision carrier, this may confound matters a bit because you will be SHIFTING into destiny, while also learning to walk in and drink the cup of these other areas. These areas also require a literal embodying of their blueprints along with drinking the cup. It will feel like double death. SIGH! The cup will feel like it is running over with the need to sacrifice self.
- You will love the supports and covenants God sets in the season of SHIFTING in your life, while being challenged with embracing the

full responsibilities, accountabilities, and enmeshing of the relationships.
- ❖ You will feel alone at times even though God sends supports and covenants as there are moments that it will only be you and Holy Spirit working matters out regarding your call.
- ❖ You will want your supports and covenants to be in the birthing room with you as you endeavor to drink the full cup but at times, there is only so far they can go with you. They will be right outside the birthing room of prayer but may not be allowed to enter into the full chamber of earnest prayer with you.
- ❖ You will feel empty at times because there is an emptying out that occurs so God can fill you up with the pure character and standards needed to sustain in your calling.
- ❖ You will feel vulnerable with your supports and covenants because you recognize you cannot live without them but flesh will not want you to lean on them. The devil will also try to isolate you and get you to not lean on them, but the soultie that God has knitted will draw you to them whether you like it or not.

All of this is being exposed so it can DIE.
- Your flesh is being sacrificed unto death.
- Your heart, mind and soul is being subjected to your spirit man.
- Your character is being crushed into the identity of God.
- Your lifestyle posture is being humbled unto the purpose of God.

Jesus continued to earnestly pray until he birthed out the death that he was about to endure, such that his spirit was ruling his actions. He died spiritually before he died naturally, so he and those he saved could live eternally. YOU MUST DRINK YOUR FULL CUP! SHIFT!

Dictionary.com defines *earnest* as:
1. serious in intention, purpose, or effort; sincerely zealous
2. showing depth and sincerity of feeling: earnest words; an earnest entreaty
3. seriously important; demanding or receiving serious attention

The birthing Jesus brought forth required a persistent travailing type of prayer. He was sweating blood type droplets. He acknowledged his thoughts and feelings and shared them with God. He did not try to hide them or negate them. He was vulnerable before God, while continuing to pray until the birthing was done in the spirit. Such a birthing can last a few hours, a few days, a few months, a season. I will say that resisting to drink the cup can prolong the process. Especially when you have entered a place of no return with Jesus. A place where he says "Oh, you will drink the cup and be baptized in affliction." This is a place where God has chosen you and has decided that your life is his.

> ***John 15:16*** *Ye have not chosen me, but I have chosen you, and ordained you, that ye should go and bring forth fruit, and that your fruit should remain: that whatsoever ye shall ask of the Father in my name, he may give it you.*

When God has decided he wants to use you, you will feel the burden of your cup until you drink it. SIGHHHHHHH! This is the reason so many are discontent and unfulfilled in the world and even in their saved life. God has chosen them, but they are doing their own thing or have only drunk a measure of their cup. But Jesus is saying, "Oh, you will drink the cup and be baptized in affliction."

Decreeing earnest prayer becomes your focus so you can drink the full cup of destiny. SHIFT!

Homework Explorations:
1. Journal in detail what you learned about from this chapter.
2. Spend time seeking God about what your full cup of destiny entails. Journal what he says.
3. Journal the transformation you need to make in your life in order to drink your full cup of destiny.
4. Spend time decreeing out the promises and prophecies God has spoken concerning your life. Use them to combat soul and demonic challenges that are hindering you from drinking your full cup of destiny. Journal your prayer experiences.

KINGDOM HEIRS! BLOODLINE BREAKERS

There is no doubt that fivefold ministry contends against generational curses, cycles, and patterns. This is because the mandate of fivefold ministry is for believers to live in the fullness of their destiny and calling. In order to achieve this,

- ✓ Curses must be broken
- ✓ Cycles and patterns must be exposed and extinguished
- ✓ Familiar spirits must be cast out
- ✓ Destiny killing spirits must be annihilated
- ✓ Family trends, cultures, and traditions that do not align with the biblical word and purpose of God must be cast down and replaced with his truth and standards

---

Kingdom heirs must understand that their role in the family is about being positioned to war and contend for the bloodline and contend for the bloodline and live a life that contends against the wickedness of the bloodline

---

If you are called to be THE ONE in the family line to deal with these matters, then your destiny just became more complex as you are what I call a "KINGDOM HEIR;" also known as a bloodline breaker.

*This information is from Dr. Taquetta Baker's book, "**Healing The Wounded Leader**."*

> ***Genesis 12:3*** *And I will bless them that bless thee, and curse him that curseth thee: and in thee shall all families of the earth be blessed.*
>
> ***Deuteronomy 5:9*** *Thou shalt not bow down thyself unto them, nor serve them: for I the LORD thy God [am] a jealous God, visiting the iniquity of the fathers upon the children unto the third and fourth [generation] of them that hate me,*
>
> ***Exodus 20:5*** *Thou shalt not bow down thyself to them, nor serve them: for I the LORD thy God [am] a jealous God, visiting the iniquity of the fathers upon the children unto the third and fourth [generation] of them that hate me.*

> *Deuteronomy 28:1-68* And it shall come to pass, if thou shalt hearken diligently unto the voice of the LORD thy God, to observe [and] to do all his commandments which I command thee this day, that the LORD thy God will set thee on high above all nations of the earth: (Read More...)
>
> *Jeremiah 17:5* Thus saith the LORD; Cursed [be] the man that trusteth in man, and maketh flesh his arm, and whose heart departeth from the LORD.
>
> *Ezekiel 18:19-22* Yet say ye, Why? doth not the son bear the iniquity of the father? When the son hath done that which is lawful and right, and hath kept all my statutes, and hath done them, he shall surely live. The soul that sinneth, it shall die. The son shall not bear the iniquity of the father, neither shall the father bear the iniquity of the son: the righteousness of the righteous shall be upon him, and the wickedness of the wicked shall be upon him. But if the wicked will turn from all his sins that he hath committed, and keep all my statutes, and do that which is lawful and right, he shall surely live, he shall not die. All his transgressions that he hath committed, they shall not be mentioned unto him: in his righteousness that he hath done he shall live.
>
> *Galatians 3:13* - Christ hath redeemed us from the curse of the law, being made a curse for us: for it is written, Cursed [is] every one that hangeth on a tree:

Kingdom heirs have been chosen by God to break curses and to defy and dismantle the culture strongholds and traditions that keep the family bound by familiar spirits and cycles; such that the blessings and works of the cross can adequately govern the family line. Many do not know this about themselves so they spend a lot of time battling familiar spirits and culture strongholds through conflicts with family members, but also within the community and region to which they minister. This warfare can be weighing and wounding, especially when the person has not grasped their full identity and purpose as it relates to combating these strongholds.

Many kingdom heirs have been assigned by God to take the place of the monarchy within their family line that keeps the family bound to demonic, traditional, and culture struggles and bondages. The devil knows this so he tries to expel the kingdom heir from the family line altogether through conflict, abuse, rejection, etc. Or the devil causes hardship, drama, and/or chaos, where the kingdom heir does not value their family line, dread being birthed into it or do not even know his or her lineage.

Often, there is no peace or resolving of issues by natural conversation, because the kingdom heir's very presence, successes, uniqueness, anointing, and advancement of the kingdom challenges the familiar spirits and cultural strongholds in the family. Just them being in the midst of family interactions or being the CHOSEN ONE causes these spirits and customs to conflict with them. Many kingdom heirs have contentious relationships with family members, are seen as the troublemaker, and are often blamed for things that are really the issues and challenges of the family members they are conflicting with. The kingdom heir is often told not to come around or stop going around their family because of these continuous challenges that they seem to stir unwarrantedly, they have no control over, is not fair, and lacks proper truth and justice. But that does not change the fact that the person is a kingdom heir and has been ordained to transform that lineage into the light of God. The assignment is still theirs to bear, and they have been given the responsibility to intercede, war, and stand in proxy for that family with their very life. Their very life becomes the watchman and gatekeeper of that lineage, and because of the choices they make, the lineage is restored in the blessings, fruit and plan of the Lord.

When we accompany being a kingdom heir with being a leader in ministry, called to a fivefold office, a vision carrier, we have a powerhouse leader. But also one who will experience a lot of hardship and wounding. Especially if they are not aware of their purpose in their family and is only focused on their purpose in ministry. The enemy uses their ignorance to wreak havoc in their lives and make them wish they were not chosen. Yet, their love for God makes them stay saved and in God's will, even though they wish they were living another life.

Examples of kingdom heirs in the bible:
- Joseph knew his purpose as a kingdom heir and restored prosperity and the blessings of God to his family lineage and to the nation of Israel.
- Moses did not know his purpose as a kingdom heir and struggled in his identity as the deliverer of the Israelites. He was angry about being a Hebrew, and about being raised as an orphan in Pharaoh's house. He did not understand the purpose of all of this

and lived in inadequacy about who he was called and destined to be.
- Jehoash was saved by an aunt from his grandmother, Athaliah, who killed all her grandchildren who were heirs to the family lineage, so that she could become king. Jehoash was hidden until he was old enough to reign as king. He was seven years old when he liberated and restored the lineage of David as governing rulership over Israel.

Kingdom heirs must understand that their role in the family is about being positioned to war and contend for the bloodline and live a life that contends against the wickedness of the bloodline. It is not about rescuing, enabling, fixing, or even being the one to witness and save their family; as that will manifest as they stand and fully live out their role as a kingdom heir. If the kingdom heir tries to rescue, fix, save, etc., their family members using natural means of witnessing, striving to resolve conflicts without the leading of the Lord, they will stir more warfare for themselves. The demonic forces within the bloodline, will just use family members to attack them. It is essential to trust the process. As you live in your daily destiny and calling with God and contend as a kingdom heir, he will reveal to you how your journey is impacting the family. You will eventually see the change in family members as the blessings of God and his standards begin to manifest in the family line, upon family members, and in your interactions with them. Please know that this happens over time, and as deliverance manifests, family members will fluctuate with being nice one moment and crazy the next moment. There will be seasons where interactions and the bloodline character and nature will appear to get better, then spirits that have been hiding will be exposed, and family members will start acting crazy again. It is important not to let your guard down until God has confirmed that a true SHIFT has come to the bloodline. It is also essential to understand that your battle is not with your family but with the demonic forces that want to keep them in bondage. Remembering this will help you to forgive quickly and to be obedient to the strategies and directions God provides regarding your family. Some of the directions will appear challenging and unfair. But overtime, you will understand them, reap the fruit of them, and see them tangibly manifest in your family line. I do suggest that as you stand, know that your fight is for the younger and future generation – generations of family members that you have not even seen and met yet. They will benefit the most from who you are as a kingdom heir. They will get to live for God and experience his blessings in ways that you and past generations did not. How awesome is that? SHIFT!

If you are a kingdom heir I encourage you to purchase my book, "Kingdom Heir Decree That Thang." I discuss this topic in detail and provide decrees and wisdom on how to stand as a bloodline breaker. SHIFT!

> *Matthew 6:33 But seek ye first the kingdom of God, and his righteousness; and all these things shall be added unto you*
>
> *Mark 10:30 But he shall receive an hundredfold now in this time, houses, and brethren, and sisters, and mothers, and children, and lands, with persecutions; and in the world to come eternal life.*

Homework Explorations:
1. Journal your thoughts on this chapter. Include ways you may be a kingdom heir. Share the experiences and dynamics that brought you to this conclusion.
2. Study the life of Joseph and Moses. Journal no less than five godly principles you learned from him as a kingdom heir.
3. Study Athalia. Journal what you learned about her demonic ways and how the enemy will seek to kill a kingdom heir.

BALANCING LIFE, DESTINY & THE VISION

Balance and self-care is essential to being healthy as you journey in destiny and as a vision carrier. Many people have trouble taking time to refresh. We tend to have a mindset that if we take time away:

- Things will not get done.
- People and duties will become stagnant or even regress.
- People and duties cannot survive and grow without us.
- We are failing or neglecting people or duties.
- We are failing God and our calling.
- We are failing the vision of our business, organization or ministry.
- We are not equipped as if we were we would not need respite.
- We are weak, as resting means we cannot handle what has been granted to our hands.

Most of our mindsets regarding resting are rooted in pride. As the focus is more about us and how our identity and self-worth is rooted in what we do, rather than who God is and what he does through us. Such a disposition is error as we constantly need to do and help in order to have a sense of value or self-importance. This is idolatry, because much of what we are doing is about building up our own kingdom, where we are glorified, rather than establishing God's kingdom where he is glorified. There is also a fear that someone will take what we have built, and even with blatant moral discrepancies, some feel they are above taking a sabbatical to be restored in God. This is pride at work as the focus is self. There is a false sense of security, and obligation in and to God, when really the person's trust and commitment is rooted in self, and in his or her accomplishments. This is a dangerous place to be because the person operates as if God is with them, when really they have left the governing of God, and are now positioned for a great fall.

> ***Proverbs 16:18*** *Pride goeth before destruction, and a haughty spirit before a fall.*

It is important to note that you will need rest and the vision will require seasons of rest. When we feel the need to steal away with God, and when God tells us to rest, he is preparing us for a greater purpose than what is currently going on around us. The enemy and people do not enter a place of rest just because we desire to, or are unctioned to by the Lord. The enemy continues to be his same old devouring self, and people continue onward with their lives and issues. During times of rest, we notice the enemy's workings and the needs of the people all the more, because our defenses are down due to a posture of rest. We are also on the outside looking in, so we are seeing what is occurring and as caregivers, our life's purpose is to step in and save the day. However, when we continue to focus on the enemy and people's issues, rather than resting and seeking a refreshing in God, we are being disobedient, and we are uncovered from the protection of God. This gives the enemy a legal right to attack us, and people the right to weary and drain what little strength we have. We must be postured in a place of knowing that as we are obedient to God, he will fortify us from the lurking enemy, and take care of the people we are to help.

One of Greek words for *rest* is *anapausis* and means:
1. intermission; by implication, recreation, rest
2. cessation of any motion, business or labour

Rest is a literal putting to death of your works. The only way to enter true rest is to cease all works, and not be drawn into battles that are not God ordained.

> *Matthew 11:28-30 Come unto me, all ye that labour and are heavy laden, and I will give you rest. Take my yoke upon you, and learn of me; for I am meek and lowly in heart: and ye shall find rest unto your souls. For my yoke is easy, and my burden is light.*

Moreover, there is a changing of guards in the place of rest. You exchange your strength and workings for God's easy yoke and burden.

God promises refuge and lightheartedness when there is a true positioning of rest. At times, we are not able to discern the refuge because resting usually manifests what is already unrested/disquieted within us. If we are anxious, agitated, murmuring, complaining, sick, tired of warring, overworked, overburdened, etc., it is usually an indication of the weariness that is already in us, and is the reason God required a time of rest in the first place.

We tend to see such irritations as being from the enemy and the enemy harassing us in our rest, but this is not the enemy. This is what needs to be cleansed out of us - exchanging our overburdened soul for a refreshing of our soul. We simply recognize these things now because we do not have people, the enemy, trials, war, duties and labor to distract us. If we really enter a place of rest, these harassments manifesting from within us will dissolve, and then the enemy will not have a foothold in our time of rest to heighten and take advantage of these open doors in our lives.

Rest is a literal putting to death of your works

Rest is a fixed and stable place or position. In this place, the leader is not wandering in and out of rest. The leader is submitted to being seated in God, and their work is centered on staying grounded and postured in this position.

> ***Psalms 91:1-2 The Amplified Bible*** *HE WHO dwells in the secret place of the Most High shall remain stable and fixed under the shadow of the Almighty [Whose power no foe can withstand]. I will say of the Lord, He is my Refuge and my Fortress, my God; on Him I lean and rely, and in Him I [confidently] trust!*

The Message Bible You who sit down in the High God's presence, spend the night in Shaddai's shadow, Say this: God, you're my refuge. I trust in you and I'm safe!

Hebrews 4:11 Let us labour therefore to enter into that rest, lest any man fall after the same example of unbelief.

The Amplified Bible Let us therefore be zealous and exert ourselves and strive diligently to enter that rest [of God, to know and experience it for ourselves], that no one may fall or perish by the same kind of unbelief and disobedience [into which those in the wilderness fell].

As we further consider *Mathew 11:28*,

Labour is *spoudazo* in Greek and means:
1. seed (used in sowing): to use speed, i. e. to make effort, be prompt or earnest, do
2. (give) diligence, be diligent (forward), endeavor, labour, study
3. due diligence, be diligent, give diligence, be forward, labour, study
4. to hasten, make haste, to exert one's self

Greek word for labor denotes that when we are diligent to enter a place of rest in God, it is seed used for sowing. We sow into being diligent to rest and God rewards us by doing or leading us in doing all the work that needs to be done in us and for us. We are totally submitted to His strength and His spirit, and do nothing of and in our own accord.

It is therefore important to have a passion in staying in this place when God is requiring it of you. Pursue it with passion like you would pursue anything that you deem important and be okay with ceasing from works, personal pulls and pulls of people, or obligations and responsibilities that will only drain you and steal your time of renewal in God.

Another Greek words for *rest* is *katapausis* and means:
1. reposing down, i. e. (by Hebraism) abode
2. a putting to rest calming of the winds, a resting place
3. metaph. the heavenly blessedness in which God dwells, and of which he has promised to make persevering believers in Christ partakers after the toils and trials of life on earth are ended

Dictionary.com defines *repose* as:
1. to lie at rest
2. to lie dead
3. to remain still or concealed
4. to take a rest
5. to rest for support: lie

As we are diligent in pursuing such a place of rest and calmness, our spiritual and natural posture should literally appear as dead. Also, unhealthy things should die in us just because we have been obedient to resting in God.

Repose suggests that this rest should be as a death. The quietness we enter should be in such submission that we appear dead from doing works. We should be totally submitted and focused on being humbled, bowed and prostrate before Jesus.

> ***Hebrews 4::12 New Living Bible*** *says: For the word of God is living and active and sharper than any double- edged sword, piercing even to the point of dividing soul from spirit, and joints from marrow; it is able to judge the desires and thoughts of the heart. And no creature is hidden from God, a but everything is naked and exposed to the eyes of him to whom we must render an account.*

This asserts that we are not trying to hide our sins, faults, or weariness, but are taking them to him - before him. As we are diligent in resting, his word goes in and surgically removes everything that is not like him. It divides the good from the bad and cleanses us (our souls), then renews and reconnects us (our spirits) in places that were disconnected from him.

> ***The Message Bible*** *God means what he says. What he says goes. His powerful Word is sharp as a surgeon's scalpel, cutting through everything, whether doubt or defense, laying us open to listen and obey. Nothing and no one is impervious to God's Word. We can't get away from it--no matter what.*

> ***The Amplified Bible*** *Let us therefore be zealous and exert ourselves and strive diligently to enter that rest [of God, to know and experience it for ourselves], that no one may fall or perish by the same kind of unbelief and disobedience [into which those in the wilderness fell]. For*

the Word that God speaks is alive and full of power [making it active, operative, energizing, and effective]; it is sharper than any two-edged sword, penetrating to the dividing line of the breath of life (soul) and [the immortal] spirit, and of joints and marrow [of the deepest parts of our nature], exposing and sifting and analyzing and judging the very thoughts and purposes of the heart.

<u>Sharper</u> is <u>tomoteros</u> in Greek and means:
1. to cut; more comprehensive or decisive than, as if by a single stroke
2. whereas that implies repeated blows, like hacking
3. more keen, sharper

<u>Homework Explorations:</u>
1. What did you learn from this chapter?
2. What reasons is rest essential to your destiny and effectiveness as a vision carrier?
3. What challenges if any do you have with resting and taking breaks?
4. List three goals you can work on to improve in taking time to refresh and truly rest inside the presence of God?

SUGGESTIONS FOR TAKING RESPITE

In addition to daily prayer and study, you should be taking weekly time to replenish before the Lord, and just for leisure purposes. Jesus encouraged the disciples in this area:

> *Mark 6:30-32* reads: *And he said unto them, Come ye yourselves apart into a desert place, and rest a while: for there were many coming and going, and they had no leisure so much as to eat.*

These wisdom keys can be implemented for short and long-term times of respite.

- Decide how much time you are going to take and stick to your regimen (e.g. A few hours, one day, three days, seven days, twenty-one days, forty days).

- If it is for a few hours, give yourself that time without feeling like you have to share it with anyone. Just take it. God knows what can occur during that time and if something happens that you need to be a part of, he will unction you. Moses was experiencing the weighty glory and instruction of the Lord and God said to him "*Go, get thee down; for thy people, which thou broughtest out of the land of Egypt, have corrupted themselves*" (*Exodus 32:7*). If you are needed, God will make sure you know.

- Establish a day just for you during the week so people will know you are off limits for that day. If your respite is for a longer period of time, let those close to you know that you will not be available for those amount of days, and to only contact you in case of emergency. If you have a ministry, let those who you oversee know you will not be available, and put someone in charge that can oversee the ministry while you are resting.

- If you are married and have children, tell your spouse of your respite plans and ask him or her to come into agreement with giving you this time of refreshing. Let the children know as well, and have them go to your spouse for whatever they need. Depending on your home environment, you may have to take respite outside of the home. Be okay with doing this. You cannot adequately be there for your family if you have nothing to give. Your family can also leave the home and give you time at home with Jesus. Some leaders have time during the day for respite, while everyone is away. It is important to schedule that time in a few days a week, where it is just you and Jesus. Be disciplined in your other duties and responsibilities, while making this a balanced priority in your life.

- Log off of all social media and messenger sites. These are an asset not a priority. If you have built a ministry through these sites, and they are rooted in the Lord, then they will keep. You do not have to operate in fear where you are deceived into believing that if you do not feed people every day, they will not follow you. They should not be drawn to you, but to the God in you. This is another avenue the enemy is draining people and leaders, and they do not recognize it. Many social media people are fickle and flighty. They feed on the next catchy word or trend, but rarely are they implementing what is spoken in their lives to produce real change. Jesus is not about tickling people's fancies. He is about saving and transforming lives. Be focused on transforming people rather than gorging them with revelation that their lives and spiritual walks cannot digest. Delete the apps off your devices if you have to. Do whatever you need to do to close in with Jesus.

- If your rest time is longer than three days, then commit to checking emails, texts, and phone call messages once a day. Only respond to what is important and immediately requires attention. Put a 30-minute time limit on this so that you are not being drawn back into works when you should be resting. Unless it is a life or death situation, delegate any other emergencies and duties to a responsible party, and return to communion with the Lord. And even with life and death situations, you must recognize that all things are in God's hands. Jesus was about his father's business when Lazarus died, and some of it included him resting and refreshing before the Lord. Jesus was challenged by Lazarus' death, how others responded to Lazarus' death, had compassion for their grief, and he also was grieved to the point of weeping. However, Jesus did not feel guilty because Lazarus died, nor did he take on the guilt others tried to put upon him. He also raised

Lazarus from the dead. You have the power to resurrect anything that dies once you return from your time of rest and being about your father's business of getting what you need from him, so you can walk in pure power and authority (***Read John 11:32-45***).

- This time of rest is for you. You are not praying for anyone else, praying for the ministry, interceding, etc., unless God leads you to do so. Otherwise, it is time for you to take yourself before God, so he can replenish and renew you.

- You may have to spend the first few minutes, hours, or days of your rest time releasing people and duties to JESUS and breaking soulties to them. *Matthew 11:28-30 says Come unto me, all ye that labour and are heavy laden, and I will give you rest. Take my yoke upon you, and learn of me; for I am meek and lowly in heart: and ye shall find rest unto your souls. For my yoke is easy, and my burden is light.* You will have to release the yoke of people, ministry, and life, and anyway you are tied and obligated to them and take on the yoke of the Lord. You will know there is an unhealthy yoke when you are trying to pray for yourself and press into Jesus, but that person, situation, concern, or duty keeps coming into your mind/heart, and drawing your attention away from you and God. Break ties with it and surrender it to the greatest hands it could be in which is Jesus. If this does not work, then search if it belongs in this time of prayer with you and Jesus. If Jesus says it does, then allow Jesus to direct you in how to pray, journal about or approach it.

- As you surrender matters to God, pursue God, repent for sin issues and character flaws, etc., and also take time to receive. So often we are talking and pressing in through a hunger and desire for a great encounter with God, until we do not realize God is with us, and is pouring himself into us. Take time in silence while just resting in the presence of the Lord. Just wait in the Lord. If he talks that is okay. If he does not talk, that is okay too. He is your friend. You do not talk to your friend the entire time you are hanging out. Sometimes you are quiet and just resting and being together. Be okay with doing this with the Lord. You do not have to gimmick and perform for God, and please do not require him to gimmick and perform for you. Wait in courage that he is with you and is enjoying rest time with you. ***Psalms 27:14*** *Wait on the Lord: be of good courage, and he shall strengthen thine heart: wait, I say, on the Lord.*

- Be okay with falling asleep. Some of you need to sleep. Sleep is spiritual, healthy, and brings healing and direction. ***Psalms 63:6*** *When I remember thee upon my bed, and meditate on thee in the night watches.* ***Psalms 4:4*** *Stand in awe, and sin not: commune with your own heart upon your bed, and be still. Selah.* ***Psalms 16:7*** *I will bless the LORD, who hath given me counsel: my reins also instruct me in the night seasons.* ***Isaiah 26:11*** *With my soul have I desired thee in the night; yea, with my spirit within me will I seek thee early: for when thy judgments are in the earth, the inhabitants of the world will learn righteousness.* At the moment you SHIFT into personal rest, you are deciding to enter a night season. You have blacked the rest of the world out and you are in a time of communion with the Lord. The only light you should be seeing is his glory light. God releases dreams, visions, instructions and strategies while we sleep. I often hear God talking to me in my sleep. He will have me get up and journal things he shares and then I will return to sleep where I am communing with him. ***Proverbs 3:24*** *When thou liest down, thou shalt not be afraid: yea, thou shalt lie down, and thy sleep shall be sweet.* When something is sweet it is pleasant, delightful, refreshing, enjoyable, joyful. This is one-way God cleanses heaviness, depression, stress, and frustration. He does it with good sleep. Sometimes you can feel the Holy Spirit healing and refreshing you as you sleep. Sometimes you are just experiencing good sound sleep. If you get sleepy, go to sleep and trust that because you took time with God, he knows what you have need of. ***Psalms 3:5*** *I lay down and slept; I awoke, for the LORD sustains me.*

- Sometimes we lie down in prayer with God and we are so engulfed in his presence that we go into a trancelike state where we feel like we cannot move. We feel like we are in between being sleep and awake. Be okay when experiencing this. God does some of his best healing and communing in this state. He is satiating and replenishing you. Satiate means "*to bathe, to satisfy, to soak, and to fill you up."* ***Jeremiah 31:25-26*** *For I have satiated the weary soul, and I have replenished every sorrowful soul. Upon this I awaked, and beheld; and my sleep was sweet unto me.* ***The Amplified Bible*** *For I will [fully] satisfy the weary soul, and I will replenish every languishing and sorrowful person. Thereupon I [Jeremiah] awoke and looked, and my [trancelike] sleep was sweet [in the assurance it gave] to me.*

- Have a journal, pen, and bible handy so you can scribe whatever God shares and study scripture as God leads. A recorder can also be beneficial if you want to record any words of prophecy, knowledge, strategy, and counsel that the Lord gives. These words will still need to be written so the vision can be engraved (imparted and established) into the earth realm, where you and others can read and utilize it. ***Isaiah 30:8*** *Now go, write it before them in a table, and note it in a man, that it may be for the time to come for ever and ever.* ***Habakkuk 2:2*** *And the LORD answered me, and said, Write the vision, and make it plain upon tables, that he may run that readeth it.*

Example Of A Personal Wellness Vision Plan

Block these times out on your calendar so you will not give this time away to anything else, and so you can be accountable to your personal wellness plan.

- Take a personal leisure day every Monday.
- Pray at 5am to 7am Tuesday - Friday (An hour of that is just you and Jesus and the other is for people and ministry).
- Saturday and Sunday are flexible.
- Fast Tuesdays and Thursdays until 6pm water only.
- Work on sermons and teachings 12pm to 2pm on Tuesdays and Thursdays
- Exercise Wednesday, Thursday, Friday at 9am for 45 minutes.
- Counseling and mentoring hours Wednesday and Saturday from 9am to 12pm and from 2pm to 5pm.
- Take a quarterly three day personal fast and consecration sabbatical where it is just time with God (March, June, September).
- Take a sabbatical the second week of November to the first week of January of the next year.

Use the suggestions and examples above to write your own personal plan for wellness and respite. Share your plan with your tribe so they can keep you accountable to maintaining self-care.

BALANCING FAMILY & RELATIONSHIPS

Balancing Dating & Engaged Relationships:
If you are dating or engaged, be honest about your ministry schedule and your times of prayer and study with the Lord. Role model your schedule, rather than giving the impression that you have free time that you do not really have. Let the person know the reason God has required the specific disciplines for you so they can pray concerning what you are sharing, and have a clear vision of who you are in God.

- Seek the Lord together for any changes you each need to make in each of your spiritual walks to make time for one another.

- Create a vision plan for cultivating your relationship and commit to working it.

- Schedule prayer and study time together. This will help with your transition if you have been single for a while, and are used to spending a lot of time praying, studying and doing ministry. This will also help you build one another up in the Lord.

- Have a balance between attending ministry activities and leisure time. Be cognizant of not just spending time together at ministry events. Schedule leisure events that you both may enjoy, but do not hinder or jeopardize your walk with the Lord.

- Communicate when you feel neglected or torn between the relationship and ministry. Encourage the other person to do the same. Commit to not holding back your thoughts and feelings in this area as it will cause an open door to division and strife. Communication is key to giving your thoughts and feelings a voice in the relationship, and to getting your needs and desires met. You must be able to communicate, because the Lord will not tell you every single thing no matter how anointed you are. This will cause you to grow in being honest and vulnerable with one another in your desires, needs, and standards.

- If you are dating or engaged, the Lord will give you grace to sustain the relationship. In busy seasons, time will be stretched. You must set aside special time for one another knowing God has given you the grace to walk in the relationship. He released the relationship in due time knowing you could balance ministry, work life, and personal relationship. Therefore, be okay with working through these seasons.

- Be able to celebrate one another. You are not in competition with one another but there to support, strengthen, and esteem each other greater than yourselves as you move forward in unity. No one wants to date or become engaged with someone who cannot genuinely celebrate their success. You must be willing to gut out any subtle jealousy, inadequacy, or revenge of wanting to perform better than your potential spouse.

- Please know that whatever you root in your foundation will be difficult to gut out in the future. It is important to have a balanced healthy foundation that your relationship can stand on.

Balancing Marriage and Family Relationships:

- Make weekly time for your marriage and family. Schedule it on your calendar and make it a priority. Ensure you schedule time for just your spouse alone, as well as the entire family. Remember to never stop dating your spouse! It is also important to confirm on a regular frequency that the scheduled time is a time that works for the family and change it as needed, but do all you can to not cancel it.

- Resist adding events to your calendar that are not a part of what God is requiring of you in the present season you are in. Make sure you communicate and share your calendar with your spouse and family, to ensure that their needs are covered during these times and/or adjustments can be made.

- Resist enabling people and having meetings where people just want to waste time, but are not about true change.

- Trust your team and promote accountability. If they cannot be accountable then replace them with someone who can. A lot of times, we keep people in positions to avoid conflict, but this is at the expense of you having to step in and do it. Replace them with someone that can be accountable, so you do not have to spend your time fulfilling duties that others can do.

- Pace yourself in your ministry vision. Be cognizant to hearing God concerning what you need to be working on at any given season, so you will not stretch yourself too thin.

- Be disciplined in scheduling meetings and completing ministry duties when other family members are busy so you all can be working at the same time, as opposed to hitting and missing one another. If there is a time that this cannot be accomplished, it is important that you communicate this to your family and be disciplined with the scheduled time.

- Invite and implement your family into your ministry endeavors and what God is doing in your life. Often we are selfish and protective in this area without realizing that it can cause family members to be jealous of your relationship with God and your ministry. It can also cause wounds and conflicts where there are demands to choose between the two. Ask your family for feedback on your ministry endeavors and be open to hearing them. This will help them feel a part of this portion of your life versus separating the two. Remember your family is your primary ministry!

- Every marriage and family is different. It is okay to consider suggestions from others, but it is best to search God for a vision plan for your marriage and family. What works for others may not work for your marriage and family. Consult with your spouse and family concerning the plan, and give them the opportunity to change and add to the plan. The vision plan can include how you desire your relationships to be, desires of spending time together, commitments to supporting one another's life events, activities and outings you all can plan and do together, and etc. Revisit the plan every few months to make sure it still works for your current family dynamics and adjust it accordingly.

- Do not try to fit ministry duties and obligations that may arise in particular seasons, inside the dynamics of your marriage and family. Take time to evaluate what season you are in with God, and share what God has said with your spouse and family. Then together you all explore with God what standards will be needed to complete the will of God, while also remaining committed to the family needs and desires.

- Text, call, and email to express affirmations of love, appreciation, support, and encouragement. Ensure that you are communicating in a fashion that fits each family members' needs. While your child may receive from a text message, your spouse may prefer a call, so they can hear your voice. Know what each family member needs and desires, and engage them accordingly. Also, make sure they are aware of your needs and desires, so they can bring fulfillment to your life.

- Consistently check on your spouse and families' well-being. Show concern for their soul with such fervor as you would those under your ministry. At no point should your family feel as if they lack priority in your life.

- Plan family vacations that are not centered around ministry. It is important that you spend time connecting and making memories with your family to ensure continued balance for both you and your family. It can be as simple as a weekend trip, or a 7-day trip. The key is you are making time to focus on them. Consider and plan separate trips for just you and your spouse, and then one with the entire family at least once a year.

- Speak into your family and make sure their spiritual needs are met. They need to see and know that you care about their spiritual growth just as much and more than those you are assigned to in the Kingdom.

Homework Explorations:
1. What areas do you need to improve in relations to balancing marriage, children, family, dating, and friendships?
2. What are the biggest challenges you have with taking personal time to be with family and friends?

3. Use the suggestions above to write a vision plan that you and your family can realistically implement into your daily lives.

BOOK REFERENCES

- *Apostolic Mantle By Taquetta Baker*

- *Blueletterbible.com*

- *Biblestudytools.com*

- *Dictionary.com*

- *Kingdom Decrees For Sustaining The Vision By Taquetta Baker*

- *Olivetree.com*

- *Pastoral Statistics Provided by The Fuller Institute, George Barna, Lifeway, Schaeffer Institute of Leadership Development, and Pastoral Care Inc. (https://www.pastoralcareinc.com/statistics/)*

- *Strongs Exhaustive Bible Concordance Online Bible Study Tools*

- *Sustaining The Vision Workbook by Taquetta Baker*

- *The US Army News & Information website (https://www.army.mil)*

- *Wikipedia*

- *Cover photo by Reenita Keys. Connect with her via Facebook.*

- *Editing by Amanda Latrice & Nina Cook Connect with them via Facebook.*